# KS2
# Science

## Practice Book

### KS2 Science
Practice Book

Jon Goulding and Jennifer Smith

# Contents

# Contents

# Asking Scientific Questions and Collecting Data

## Challenge 1

**1** When planning an enquiry, which of the following are important parts of the process? Tick **two**.

guessing the answer ☐     writing the method ☑

choosing the equipment ☑     selecting the temperature ☐

*1 mark*

**2** Write the correct unit of measure to use for measuring each of the following.

temperature of a room       _____°/° _____

length of the stem of a plant _____ cm _____

volume of water       _____ ml _____

*2 marks*

**3** What equipment would you use to measure each of the following?

temperature of a room       _____ 10 _____

length of the stem of a plant _____ cm _____

volume of water       _____ ml _____

*2 marks*

Marks.......... /5

## Challenge 2

**1** Darcy thinks that the surface area of a container might affect how quickly water evaporates. She poses the question she wants to answer: 'Do bigger containers make water evaporate more quickly?' Improve this question, using what Darcy already thinks to help you.

_____

_____

*1 mark*

**2** Explain how Darcy should make sure her enquiry is a fair test.

_____

_____

_____

*2 marks*

Marks.......... /3

# Asking Scientific Questions and Collecting Data

## Challenge 3

**1** During her enquiry, Darcy uses three different containers. Two are drawn below. Draw what a third container might look like.

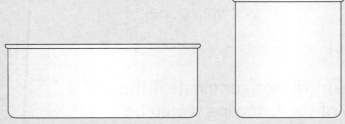

**2** Explain what Darcy should do to ensure that the data she collects is accurate.

_____

_____

**3** Darcy decided to record her data in the table on the right.

Complete the table using the following information:

| Container surface area (cm²) | Volume of water evaporated (ml) |
|---|---|
| 9 | |
| 15 | |
| | |

14 ml evaporated from the smallest surface area and 35 ml from the largest. The surface area of 15 cm² lost 23 ml of water through evaporation. The largest container had a surface area of 24 cm².

**4** Darcy wants to conduct another enquiry about evaporation. She poses the question: 'How does temperature affect the rate of evaporation of water?'

Write a short method for Darcy, explaining how she could make her enquiry a fair test.

_____

_____

_____

Marks.......... /8

Total marks ............. /16          How am I doing?

# Making Conclusions and Using Evidence

## Challenge 1

**1** Which of the following refers to the conclusion of an enquiry? Tick **one**.

the data ☐   how it was done ☐

a summary of the findings ☐

*1 mark*

**2** If an enquiry concludes that a bean will not germinate if the temperature is below 0°C, which of the following would be a reasonable next question? Tick **two**.

Do other seeds germinate below 0°C? ☐

Can beans grow in the cold? ☐

What is the lowest temperature at which beans will germinate? ☐

*2 marks*

Marks.........../3

## Challenge 2

**1** An enquiry to find how much a sunflower would grow over one week at different temperatures produced the following data.

| Temperature (°C) | Height of plant (cm) |
|---|---|
| 7 | 6 |
| 14 | 15 |
| 21 | 26 |

What information does the data give about the effect of temperature on sunflower growth?

_____

_____

*2 marks*

**2** Write an appropriate 'next question' based on the findings of the enquiry above.

_____

*1 mark*

Marks.........../3

# Making Conclusions and Using Evidence

**Challenge 3**

**1** Lena wants to know how her heart rate changes when she rests after exercise. She runs as fast as she can for one minute, then uses a heart rate monitor to measure her heart rate in BPM (beats per minute). She then records her heart rate every 30 seconds for three minutes. The graph below shows her results.

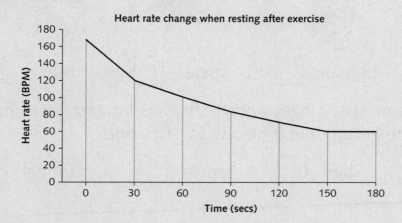

Heart rate change when resting after exercise

**a)** What does the graph tell us about the evidence that Lena has found about her heart rate during rest after exercise?

_____

1 mark

**b)** Write a conclusion for Lena.

_____

_____

1 mark

**c)** Write two questions Lena might ask for new enquiries to help her understand more about her heart rate and exercise.

_____

_____

2 marks

Marks.......... /4

Total marks ............. /10          How am I doing?

# Grouping Living Things

## Challenge 1

**1** What do vertebrates have that invertebrates do not have?

_____

**2** Which animal is an invertebrate? Tick **one**.

horse ☐          human ☐          spider ☐          fish ☐

**3** On her farm, Anna sees a baby animal that has fur and drinks milk. Which vertebrate group does it belong to? Tick **one**.

amphibian ☐          bird ☐          reptile ☐          mammal ☐

Marks.........../3

## Challenge 2

**1** A visitor to school shows the children a fish and a snake.

What features do the fish and snake have in common? Tick **two**.

both have gills ☐          both have scales ☐

both lay eggs ☐          both have lungs ☐

**2** The visitor shows the children three possible reasons why we sort animals into different groups. Write **true** or **false** next to each reason.

It helps animals be safe.          _____

It helps to identify animals.          _____

It helps animals to feed.          _____

**3** The children are shown an insect. Name **two** characteristics it will have.

_____          _____

Marks.........../5

# Grouping Living Things

**Challenge 3**

1   What are the three main groups of living things?

_____     _____     _____

3 marks

2   Give an example of a micro-organism and give one key characteristic.

_____

_____

2 marks

3   We can classify plants into one of two groups. What are these groups known as?

_____     _____

2 marks

4   Give at least two similarities and two differences between birds and reptiles.

| Similarities | Differences |
| --- | --- |
|  |  |

3 marks

5   Use the branched key below to identify each of the vertebrates. Place the letter **A, B, C, D** or **E** next to each picture.

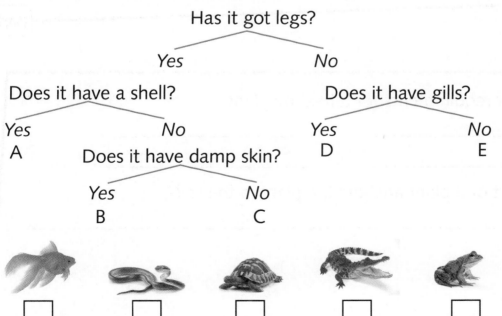

3 marks

Marks......... /13

Total marks ............. /21        How am I doing?   😊   😐   😣

# Parts of Plants

## Challenge 1

**1** Label this diagram of a plant.

[diagram of a plant with four empty label boxes]

2 marks

**2** Which part of a flowering plant attracts insects?

root ☐      leaves ☐      flower ☐      stem ☐

1 mark

Marks.........../3

## Challenge 2

**1** Name **four** requirements for a healthy plant.

_____        _____

_____        _____

2 marks

**2** Which part of a plant anchors the plant in the soil?

_____

1 mark

Marks.........../3

# Parts of Plants

## Challenge 3

**1** In which part of the plant is food made?

_____

**2** Explain how a plant gets water and nutrients to its leaves. In your explanation, make sure you name the two most important parts of the plant in this process.

_____

_____

**3** What is the difference between the root and the shoot as they grow from a germinating seed?

_____

**4** Which of the plants below should be most healthy after one week? Explain your answer.

| PLANT A | PLANT B |
|---|---|
| Temperature – normal | Temperature – normal |
| Water – daily | Water – daily |
| Light – none | Light – normal |

| PLANT C | PLANT D |
|---|---|
| Temperature – very cold | Temperature – normal |
| Water – daily | Water – none |
| Light – normal | Light – normal |

_____

_____

Marks.......... /7

Total marks ............. /13          How am I doing?

# Life Cycles

## Challenge 1

**1** In the life cycle of a frog, what is the name given to the 'baby' that hatches from an egg?

_____

1 mark

**2** What is the name given to the developing baby inside a mammal?

_____

1 mark

Marks............/2

## Challenge 2

**1** Label the stages in the life cycle of a butterfly.

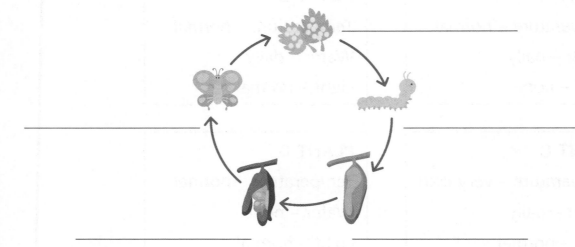

3 marks

**2** What is the main difference in the early stages of the life cycle of a mammal when compared to other animals?

_____

_____

1 mark

Marks.........../4

# Life Cycles

**Challenge 3**

**1**  In the human life cycle, what develops into an embryo?

_____

1 mark

**2**  Explain why animals and plants have a life cycle.

_____

_____

2 marks

**3**  Add the missing stages to the life cycle of each animal.

Human: foetus → _____ → child → _____ → adult

Insect:  egg  → larva  → _____ → adult

Bird:   egg  → embryo → _____ → adult

4 marks

**4**  Draw a labelled diagram to show the life cycle of an amphibian.

3 marks

Marks......... /10

Total marks ............. /16          How am I doing?

# Reproduction

## Challenge 1

1 Where are the reproductive organs of a flowering plant found?

_____

1 mark

2 The male part of the flower is the s_____ and the

female part is the c_____.

1 mark

3 In animals, the egg from the woman is fertilised by _____

from the man.

1 mark

Marks............/3

## Challenge 2

1 Why are insects an important part of reproduction in flowering
plants?

_____

1 mark

2 When pollen joins an egg in a plant, and a sperm joins with an egg
in an animal, what is the name of this process?

_____

1 mark

3 Name **two** different ways in which seeds can be dispersed so they
have room to germinate and grow.

_____        _____

2 marks

Marks............/4

# Reproduction

## Challenge 3

**1** Look at the images below. Label them 1, 2 and 3 to show the order they should be in, starting with the earliest stage.

 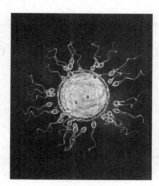 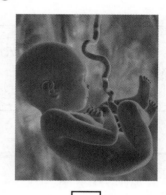

☐ ☐ ☐

1 mark

**2** Explain what has happened in stage 1 above.

_____

_____

2 marks

**3** Label the stigma, anther, stamen and carpel on the diagram below.

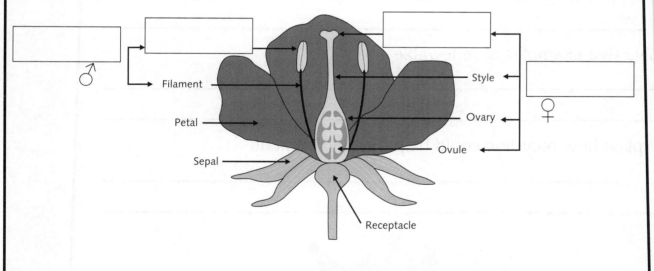

♂

Filament

Petal

Sepal

Style

Ovary

Ovule

Receptacle

♀

4 marks

Marks.......... /7

Total marks ............. /14          How am I doing?

# Changing Environments

## Challenge 1

**1** **True** or **false**? Seasons cause changes to habitats during the course of a year.

_____

1 mark

**2** What is the name given when something harmful enters the environment?

_____

1 mark

Marks............/2

## Challenge 2

**1** Give **three** examples of how humans can have a negative impact on the environment.

_____

_____

_____

3 marks

**2** Give **two** examples of renewable energy.

_____

_____

2 marks

**3** Explain how recycling could help the environment.

_____

_____

1 mark

Marks.........../6

# Changing Environments

**Challenge 3**

1   In what way do deforestation and building have a negative impact on habitats?

_____

_____

1 mark

2   Give **two** examples of how humans pollute the environment.

_____

_____

2 marks

3   Explain the environmental benefits of creating a habitat such as a garden pond.

_____

_____

1 mark

4   How can using renewable sources of energy help the environment?

_____

1 mark

Marks.........../5

Total marks ............../13          How am I doing?

1   You are asked to measure how quickly water heats in different-coloured beakers when left in the Sun. What equipment would you need?

_____

1 mark

2   How would you make sure that the enquiry described above is a fair test?

_____

_____

1 mark

3   The table below shows the percentage of cress seeds germinating in different conditions over a period of four days. The seeds were placed on cotton wool with the amount of water changed for each sample.

| Amount of water | None – dry | Slightly damp | Wet |
|---|---|---|---|
| Seed germinating | 0% | 22% | 99% |

Assuming all variables were the same, apart from the amount of water, what can you conclude from the data?

_____

_____

2 marks

4   How could the reliability of the data above be improved?

_____

1 mark

5   When pollen sticks to the stigma, what is the process known as?

_____

1 mark

18

**6**   Name **two** different ways in which seeds can be dispersed.

_____

**7**   Why is it important that seeds germinate away from the plant from which they came?

_____

**8**   The table below shows the cooling of boiling (100°C) water in plastic beakers over 30 minutes. The enquiry was trying to find out which material wrapped around each beaker was the best thermal insulator (i.e. which kept the water warmest).

| Time | 5 min | 10 min | 15 min | 20 min | 25 min | 30 min |
|---|---|---|---|---|---|---|
| **Foam Temp (°C)** | 90 | 83 | 75 | 68 | 62 | 55 |
| **Foil Temp (°C)** | 89 | 80 | 69 | 57 | 44 | 32 |
| **Paper Temp (°C)** | 87 | 78 | 65 | 52 | 40 | 27 |

**a)**   Explain which material appears to be the best thermal insulator. Why do you think this?

_____

_____

**b)**   The foil and paper were wrapped around the beakers to a thickness of 1 mm. The foam had a thickness of 1 cm. Explain why this was not a fair test, and how it could be changed to make it fair.

_____

_____

**9** Give **three** examples of how humans can help protect plant and animal habitats.

_____

_____

_____

*3 marks*

**10** Explain the difference between how mammals and reptiles are born.

_____

_____

*1 mark*

**11** What happens during fertilisation in a flowering plant?

_____

_____

*2 marks*

**12** What happens during fertilisation in vertebrates?

_____

_____

*2 marks*

**13** What are the male and female parts of a plant called?

Male _____

Female _____

*1 mark*

*1 mark*

**14** Why are leaves important to a plant?

_____

1 mark

**15** Explain how water is transported from the soil to the leaves of a plant.

_____

_____

_____

3 marks

**16** If an enquiry is trying to find the best temperature for growing tomatoes, what variable must be changed?

_____

1 mark

Marks........ /27

# Food Chains

## Challenge 1

**1** Circle the correct answer. Most food chains start with:

an animal          a green plant          prey

*1 mark*

**2** Complete the sentences.
In a food chain:

**a)** a plant is called a _____ because it can make its own food.

**b)** an animal is called a _____ because it cannot make its own food.

*2 marks*

**3** Match the definitions to the correct answers.

| An animal that kills and eats another animal. | | Prey |
|---|---|---|
| An animal that is hunted and eaten by a predator. | | Predator |

*1 mark*

**Marks.......... /4**

## Challenge 2

**1** A hawk eats a vole, which had eaten a caterpillar, which had eaten a dandelion leaf. Construct a food chain, on a separate sheet of paper, using this information.

*2 marks*

**2** What is the producer in your food chain?

_____

*1 mark*

**3** Which animals are predators in your food chain?

_____

*2 marks*

**Marks.......... /5**

# Food Chains

**Challenge 3**

Use the food web to help you answer the following questions.

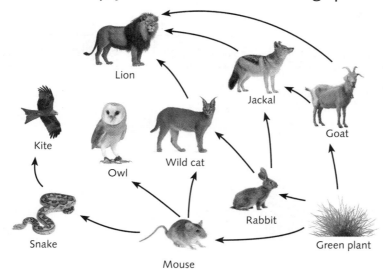

1   The lion is a predator in more than one food chain. Name **two** of the lion's prey.

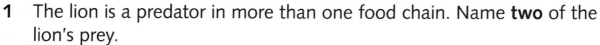

2 marks

2   Which **three** animals are both predators and prey?

3 marks

3   Predict which animals would be most affected if the numbers of mice decreased. Explain your thinking.

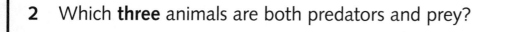

3 marks

4   Create a food chain, on a separate sheet of paper, which starts with the green plant and ends with the lion. Make sure you use arrows correctly.

2 marks

Marks......... /10

Total marks ............ /19          How am I doing?

# Digestion

1   Use the words provided to label the organs of the digestive system. Two organs have been done for you.

| small intestine | stomach | oesophagus | tongue and teeth |

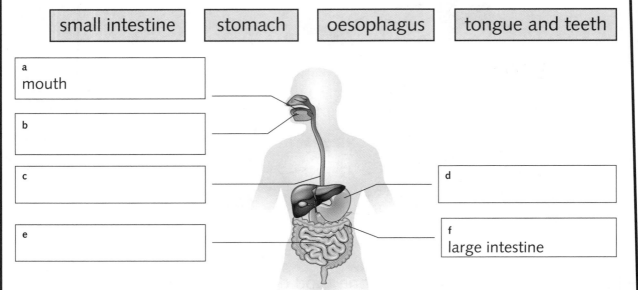

a
mouth

b

c

d

e

f
large intestine

4 marks

2   Write the types of teeth into the sentences below so that the statements are correct. Use the diagram to help you to remember.

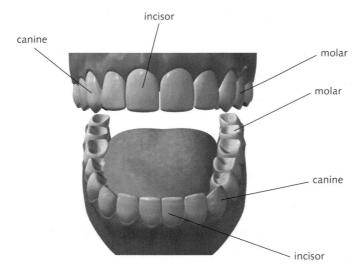

a)   The _____ teeth rip and tear foods like meat.

b)   _____ are larger flatter teeth used for crushing and grinding food.

2 marks

Marks.......... /6

24

# Digestion

## Challenge 2

**1** What is the job of the digestive system? Tick **two** statements that are correct.

To transport oxygen around the body ☐

To break down food ☐

To absorb water and nutrients into the body ☐

To support the muscles ☐

*2 marks*

**2** What is the job of the teeth and tongue in the digestive system?

_____

*2 marks*

Marks.......... /4

## Challenge 3

**1** How does the digestive system help humans to stay healthy?

_____

_____

*2 marks*

**2** Put the processes of the digestive system in the correct order by numbering them 1–5. The first one has been done for you.

The intestines break food down and absorb water and nutrients. ☐

Food enters the body through the mouth. ☐ 1

The stomach churns up food and mixes it with enzymes. ☐

The teeth and tongue break food into smaller pieces. ☐

Food is transported down the oesophagus into the stomach. ☐

*4 marks*

Marks.......... /6

Total marks ............ /16          How am I doing?  ☺  😐  😣

25

# Skeleton and Muscles

## Challenge 1

**1** Which part of the body protects the brain?

_____

1 mark

**2** Tick **three** functions of the skeleton.

Supporting the body ☐     Transporting blood ☐

Protecting organs ☐     Supporting movement ☐

3 marks

**3** Using the words provided, label the skeleton correctly.

| pelvis | ribs | skull | spine | kneecap |

**a**

**b**

**c**

**d**

**e**

5 marks

Marks.......... /9

# Skeleton and Muscles

## Challenge 2

**1** Which part of the skeleton protects:

**a)** the heart? _____
**b)** the pelvic organs? _____

**c)** the spinal cord? _____

3 marks

**2** Using the words provided, complete the sentences correctly.

| muscles | tendons | contracts | move |
|---|---|---|---|

_____ are attached to the bones by _____. They work in pairs to help the body _____. When one muscle _____ the other one relaxes.

4 marks

**3** Name an animal that does not have a skeleton. _____

1 mark

Marks.......... /8

## Challenge 3

**1** This image shows the names of the leg muscles used to help kick a ball.

Describe how the muscles in the leg help to kick a ball.

_____

_____

_____

Quadriceps

Hamstrings

3 marks

**2** The human skeleton is not one solid piece, but many bones held together at the joints. Why are these joints so important and what would happen if human skeletons didn't have them?

_____

_____

_____

2 marks

Marks.......... /5

Total marks ............ /22     How am I doing?

# Heart and Blood Vessels

## Challenge 1

1   What are the organs and processes that deliver oxygen, nutrients and water around the body known as? Tick **one**.

digestive system ☐                    circulatory system ☐

solar system ☐

1 mark

2   Blood transports oxygen around the body and helps to eliminate carbon dioxide. **True** or **false**? _____

1 mark

3   Use the words provided to label the parts of the human heart.

| Valve | Atrium | Ventricle |

3 marks

Marks.......... /5

## Challenge 2

1   Blood transports oxygen and nutrients around the body.

   **a)** What is the blood transported around the body through?

   _____

   1 mark

   **b)** Name all **three** types of them.

   _____   _____   _____

   3 marks

2   Before blood is pumped around the body, it needs to eliminate carbon dioxide and collect oxygen. Where does this happen?

   _____

   1 mark

3   What is the function of the valves in the heart?

   _____

   1 mark

Marks.......... /6

# Heart and Blood Vessels

**Challenge 3**

**1** Joe's football team are doing a fitness test. Before they start playing, they all check their heart rates (how fast their hearts are beating). They also check their heart rates after they have been playing and running around.

**a)** How could they check their heart rate?

_____

1 mark

**b)** What is likely to happen to their heart rates when they have been playing football for a few minutes? Why?

_____

_____

_____

3 marks

**2** Joe's heart rate before the game was 60 bpm (beats per minute). At the end of the game, it had risen to 180 bpm. After the match, Joe sits down and measures his heart rate every 2 minutes for 10 minutes.

Draw a line to complete the chart to show what you think will happen to Joe's heart rate in this time.

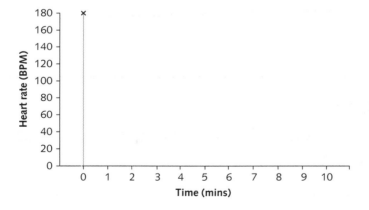

2 marks

Marks.......... /6

**Total marks** ............. /17     How am I doing?

# Healthy Living

## Challenge 1

1   Tick **two** things that can help to keep the body healthy.

smoking cigarettes ☐ exercise ☐

a balanced diet ☐ watching television ☐

2 marks

2   Complete the table using the words/phrases provided.

| Butter | Vitamins and minerals for healthy cells | Fish |

| Food | What it provides for the body |
| --- | --- |
| Berries | |
| | Fats for energy |
| | Protein for growth and repair |

3 marks

3   Sam only ever eats bread and butter. Is this a healthy, balanced diet? Why/why not?

_____

_____

2 marks

Marks.......... /7

## Challenge 2

1   Billy is trying to stay healthy.

a)  Other than eating a balanced diet, name **two** things he can do to keep his body healthy.

_____

_____

2 marks

b)  He does not like fruit or vegetables. What will his body be missing out on if he doesn't eat them?

_____

1 mark

c)  Why are these nutrients important for the body?

_____

1 mark

# Healthy Living

**2** Billy loves to play football, and believes it is a good way to stay fit and healthy.

   **a)** Is he correct? _____

   **b)** What benefits does playing football have for the body? Name **two**.

   _____

   _____

1 mark

2 marks

Marks.......... /7

## Challenge 3

Children at Northbank Primary School are learning about healthy lifestyles. They conduct a survey of local adults, and the results are shown in the table below.

| Adult | Exercises regularly | Smokes cigarettes | Eats a balanced diet |
|---|---|---|---|
| A | Yes | Yes | Yes |
| B | Yes | No | Yes |
| C | No | No | No |
| D | No | Yes | No |

**1** Which adult is most likely to have a healthy heart? Why?

_____

2 marks

**2** Which adult is most likely to have problems with their health? Why?

_____

2 marks

**3** What advice would you give to adult A to help them improve their health? Why?

_____

_____

_____

3 marks

Marks.......... /7

Total marks ............ /21          How am I doing?

# Adaptation and Variation

## Challenge 1

**1** An animal's offspring will be identical to its biological parents. **True** or **false**?

_____

**2** Circle **two** characteristics that a person may inherit from their biological parents.

| A love of music | | Hair colour | | How tall they are |

**3** Most living things have special characteristics which help them to survive in their environment. What do we call these special changes or characteristics?

_____

Marks.......... /4

## Challenge 2

**1** Give **one** example of how humans have adapted to survive in different or extreme environments.

_____

**2** Give **one** example of how a polar bear is adapted to live in the cold and explain what the adaptation does for the bear.

_____

**3** A duck has webbed feet, waterproof feathers and strong wings. Which **two** of these characteristics are useful for swimming in a pond?

_____        _____

Marks.......... /5

# Adaptation and Variation

1   Anna has just started at school, and everyone tells her that she looks identical to her older sister Lucy. Why is this not possible?

_____

_____

2 marks

2   Alfie is looking at old photos of his grandparents, and he notices that he has the same shaped nose as his grandfather. Is it possible that he does have the same shaped nose? Explain your answer.

_____

_____

2 marks

3   Unlike cacti, waterlilies have large, bowl-shaped leaves instead of needle-like leaves. How have their environments led to these differences in adaptations?

_____

_____

2 marks

Marks.......... /6

Total marks ............. /15     How am I doing?

# Evidence for Evolution

## Challenge 1

**1** What is the scientific theory of how living things have changed over millions of years known as? Tick **one**.

Variation ☐      Evolution ☐      Inheritance ☐

1 mark

**2** The habitat or environment of a plant or animal affects the way that it adapts and evolves. **True** or **false**?

_____

1 mark

**3** Nadia believes that humans have always been exactly as they are today; Tommy thinks that humans have evolved. Who is correct?

_____

1 mark

**4** What is the name used to describe the remains or impressions of living things which are imprinted in rocks? Tick **one**.

Rocks ☐          Fossils ☐

Minerals ☐          Skeletons ☐

1 mark

Marks.......... /4

## Challenge 2

**1** Ayumi is new to Class 6 and has never heard of evolution.

**a)** How would you explain and describe what evolution is?

_____

_____

2 marks

**b)** Why do living things need to evolve?

_____

_____

2 marks

Marks.......... /4

# Evidence for Evolution

**Challenge 3**

1   Look at the images below. One is the fossil of an Archaeopteryx
    (a winged dinosaur) and the other is a skeleton of a modern bird.

a)  What similarities can you see between the Archaeopteryx and
    the bird? Give **two**.

    _____

    _____

2 marks

b)  What difference can you see?

    _____

1 mark

c)  What conclusion could be drawn from the similarities?

    _____

    _____

1 mark

Marks.........../4

Total marks ............. /13        How am I doing?

# Solids, Liquids and Gases

## Challenge 1

**1** Label each of the pictures below as solid, liquid or gas.

**a)**

**b)**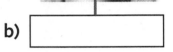

**c)**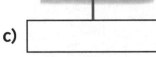

1 mark

**2** What change of state is happening in the picture below?

_____

1 mark

Marks............/2

## Challenge 2

**1** Explain why washing is hung outside on a dry day.

_____

_____

_____

_____

_____

2 marks

**2** Which of these materials will not hold their shape if transferred to a different shaped container?

wood      oil      oxygen      rock

2 marks

Marks.........../4

36

# Solids, Liquids and Gases

## Challenge 3

**1** Label the *States of Matter* diagram below using arrows and the given words.

| evaporation | condensation | melting | freezing |
|---|---|---|---|

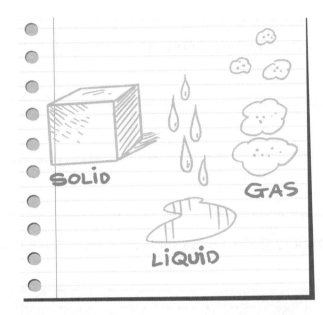

2 marks

**2** Explain what happens to form condensation on a window.

_____

_____

2 marks

**3** A class wanted to find the answer to the following question: Is the starting and final amount of water the same when water changes state from liquid, to solid and back again?

Explain the method they could use for this enquiry.

_____

_____

_____

3 marks

Marks.........../7

Total marks ............../13          How am I doing?

# The Water Cycle

## Challenge 1

1 What is the scientific name for rain and snow?

evaporation ☐          condensation ☐          precipitation ☐

*1 mark*

2 **True** or **false**? Clouds are formed by evaporation.

_____

*1 mark*

3 **True** or **false**? Washing dries more quickly on a dry day if it is warmer.

_____

*1 mark*

Marks............/3

## Challenge 2

1 Match each of the following statements to the correct process from the water cycle.

precipitation

As water vapour rises it cools and starts to form clouds.

condensation

As water is heated, water vapour rises from its surface.

evaporation

When the clouds can no longer hold the water, it falls to the ground.

*2 marks*

2 Explain what is happening when a puddle dries up.

_____

_____

*1 mark*

Marks............/3

# The Water Cycle

**1** Label and explain the water cycle diagram below.

_____

_____

_____

_____

 3 marks

**2** A class is investigating how much water evaporates from a beaker as the temperature of the water increases over a 5-hour period. Their results are shown in the table below.

| Temperature (°C) | 5 | 10 | 15 | 20 | 25 |
|---|---|---|---|---|---|
| Amount of water evaporated per hour (ml) | 4 | 9 | 13 | 16 | 19 |

What do their results tell them about how quickly the water evaporates?

_____

_____

 2 marks

Marks.........../5

Total marks .............../11          How am I doing?

# Progress Test 2

1 In a food chain, what type of living thing is usually the producer?

______________________________________________ 1 mark

2 Give an example of an animal that is a predator.

______________________________________________ 1 mark

3 Look at these adaptations. Circle the **three** that would help a cactus survive in a hot desert.

Waxy skin | Long deep roots | Bowl-shaped flowers

Long stems | Small needle-like leaves | Large flat leaves

3 marks

4 Peppered moths adapted and evolved quickly through a process of natural selection after their environment rapidly changed. What is natural selection and how does it help living things to evolve?

______________________________________________

______________________________________________

______________________________________________ 2 marks

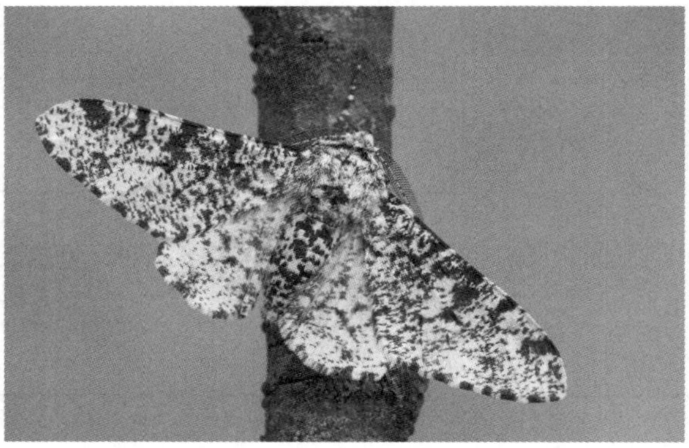

**5** Large predators, like lions, have developed lots of big sharp teeth instead of lots of different types of teeth like humans. Explain why.

_____

_____

_____

2 marks

**6** Match the type of tooth to its function.

| Canine | | Cut and slice food |
| Molar | | Tear and rip food |
| Incisor | | Crush and grind food |

3 marks

**7** The skeleton is not one solid piece but lots of different bones. How are the bones held together?

_____

1 mark

**8** Describe how both the skeleton and the muscles work together to help the body move.

_____

_____

_____

3 marks

**9** Name the **three** main parts of the circulatory system.

_____

_____

3 marks

**10** Mrs Evans is explaining the theory of evolution to her class. She uses the word ancestor a number of times. What does the word ancestor mean?

_____

_____

1 mark

**11** The stomach, oesophagus and intestines are all part of the same system in the body.

   **a)** Which system are they a part of?

   _____

                                        1 mark

   **b)** What is the job of this system?

   _____

                                          1 mark

**12** Write a different material for each state of matter.

| Solid | Liquid | Gas |
|-------|--------|-----|
|       |        |     |
|       |        |     |

_3 marks_

**13 a)** What happens during the process of evaporation?

   _____

_1 mark_

   **b)** Explain one way in which evaporation can be useful in everyday life.

   _____

_1 mark_

**14** During the weekend, Betina is very busy. She goes on a bike ride, paints a picture for her teacher, walks her dog and watches television.

   **a)** Which **two** of her activities are a form of exercise?

   _____

_1 mark_

   **b)** Give **two** ways in which Betina's body will benefit from the exercise.

   _____

   _____

_2 marks_

# Answers

**Pages 4–5**

**Challenge 1**

1. 1 mark for both answers correct: writing the method, choosing the equipment (1)
2. 1 mark for 2 correct answers, 2 marks for all three: temperature = °C, length = cm or mm, volume = ml or l (2)
3. 1 mark for 2 correct answers, 2 marks for all three: temperature = thermometer, length = ruler, volume = measuring jug/cylinder (2)

**Challenge 2**

1. Answer should include reference to the surface area of the water and how quickly it evaporates.
   e.g. Does the surface area of water in a container affect the rate of evaporation? (1)
2. The only variable Darcy should change is the surface area of the water (by using different shaped containers) (1). Other variables (e.g. the volume of water, the temperature and the location) should remain constant (1). (2)

**Challenge 3**

1. Drawing should show a container with a different-sized opening from the other two. (1)
2. She should observe and measure carefully. (1)
3.

| Container surface area (cm²) | Volume of water evaporated (ml) |
|---|---|
| 9 | 14 |
| 15 | 23 |
| 24 | 35 |

(2)

4. Method should include reference to: changing the temperature of each sample (the only variable that should change) (1); keeping other variables the same, e.g. volume of water, container and surface area of water (1); recording the start and end volume of water in each sample (1); recording the temperature of each sample (1). (4)

**Pages 6–7**

**Challenge 1**

1. a summary of the findings (1)
2. 1 mark for each correct answer: Do other seeds germinate below 0°C? What is the lowest temperature at which beans will germinate? (2)

**Challenge 2**

1. 2 marks for an answer which acknowledges that the height of the plant increased with increasing temperature AND that the most growth over a week was at a temperature of 21°C, and/or that at this temperature sunflowers grow more quickly than at lower temperatures. (1 mark for just one of these points.) (2)
2. Example answers: At what temperature do sunflowers grow the fastest? Do sunflowers continue to grow taller with increasing temperature? (1)

**Challenge 3**

1. a) It shows that, when resting after exercise, her heart rate slows. (1)

b) Following exercise, Lena's heart rate reduces over time. It decreases more slowly with increasing time and takes 150 seconds to return to a steady heart rate. (1)

c) 1 mark for each appropriate question. Example questions: How quickly does heart rate increase during exercise? Does recovery time change depending on the intensity of exercise? (2)

**Pages 8–9**

**Challenge 1**

1. a backbone (1)
2. spider (1)
3. mammal (1)

**Challenge 2**

1. 1 mark for each correct answer: both have scales, both lay eggs (2)
2. 1 mark for all three correct: false, true, false (1)
3. 1 mark for each correct answer: six legs, three body parts (2)

**Challenge 3**

1. 1 mark for each correct answer: plants, animals, micro-organisms (3)
2. 1 mark for each correct answer: bacteria (accept fungi, algae, protozoa or viruses), very small (2)
3. 1 mark for each correct answer: flowering plants, non-flowering plants (2)
4. 2 marks for one similarity and one difference, 3 marks for two of each, for example:
   Similarities – vertebrates, lay eggs, have lungs
   Differences – birds have feathers, reptiles have scales, birds can fly, birds have legs, birds have a steady body temperature, reptiles have a changing body temperature (3)
5. 1 mark for 2 correct, 2 marks for 3 correct, 3 marks for all 5 correct:
   A – Tortoise     B – frog     C – crocodile
   D – fish     E – snake (3)

**Pages 10–11**

**Challenge 1**

1. 1 mark for 2 or 3 labelled correctly, 2 marks for all 4 labelled correctly.

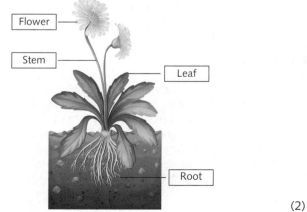

Flower
Stem
Leaf
Root

(2)

2. flower (1)

# Answers

## Challenge 2
**1** 1 mark for 2 or 3 correct answers, 2 marks for 4 correct answers: Any from – light, water, air, room, nutrients (2)
**2** the root (1)

## Challenge 3
**1** the leaves (1)
**2** 2 marks for an answer which references the root and the stem, and water and nutrients being absorbed by the roots and travelling up through the stem to the leaves. 1 mark for just one part of this. Example answer: The roots absorb water and nutrients which then travel up through the stem of the plant to the leaves. (2)
**3** The answer must acknowledge that the roots grow in search of water/nutrients while the shoot grows towards a source of light. (Accept roots grow down, shoots grow up from the germinating seed.) (1)
**4** 1 mark for correctly acknowledging Plant B as the healthiest. An additional 2 marks for reference to the plant having the best conditions for growth – a normal temperature, regular water and light. (3)

## Pages 12–13
### Challenge 1
**1** tadpole (1)
**2** foetus (accept embryo) (1)

### Challenge 2
**1** 1 mark for 2 labelled correctly, 2 marks for 3 labelled correctly, 3 marks for all labelled correctly. (3)

**2** In mammals the baby develops inside its mother and is born live whereas most other animals lay eggs in which the offspring develops. (1)

### Challenge 3
**1** a fertilised egg (1)
**2** 1 mark for one of the following, 2 marks for both: an answer which acknowledges that old plants and animals die so new ones are needed to replace them, and that it ensures the survival of the species. (2)
**3** 1 mark for each correct word given:
Human – baby, adolescent; Insect – pupa (or chrysalis); Bird – hatchling (or chick) (4)

**4** 3 marks for a diagram showing egg (or egg mass or spawn), tadpole (tadpole with legs may also be added here but is not necessary for the marks), froglet, frog. 2 marks for 3 of these in the correct order, 1 mark for 2 of these in the correct order. (3)

## Pages 14–15
### Challenge 1
**1** in the flower (1)
**2** 1 mark for both stamen and carpel (1)
**3** sperm (1)

### Challenge 2
**1** They carry pollen from male parts to female parts. (1)
**2** fertilisation (1)
**3** 1 mark each for any two from: wind, animals (sticking to them or in excrement/poo), explosion or water (2)

### Challenge 3
**1** 1 mark for correct order of: 1. fertilised egg, 2. foetus, 3. baby (1)
**2** 2 marks for an explanation referring to sperm having fertilised the egg. 1 mark for 'fertilisation'. (2)
**3** 1 mark for each correctly labelled part. (4)

## Pages 16–17
### Challenge 1
**1** True (1)
**2** pollution (1)

### Challenge 2
**1** 1 mark each for any three examples of human impact: e.g. deforestation, building, soil pollution, air pollution, plastic waste, litter, water pollution. (3)
**2** 1 mark each for any two examples of renewable energy: e.g. wind power, solar, hydroelectric, tidal, geothermal (2)
**3** The answer should refer to reduction of waste by turning waste into new objects or re-using objects. (1)

### Challenge 3
**1** 1 mark for an answer which acknowledges that deforestation and building destroy animal and plant habitats. (1)
**2** 1 mark each for any two of: air pollution (accept smoke or burning fossil fuels), water pollution, litter, plastic waste, noise, light. (2)
**3** Answer should acknowledge that it provides a safe habitat for plants and animals which live in and around ponds. (1)
**4** Answer should acknowledge that renewable sources of energy create less pollution. (1)

## Pages 18–21
### Progress Test 1
1   1 mark for at least two of: different-coloured beakers, stopwatch, thermometer.   (1)
2   1 mark for an answer which acknowledges that the only variable that should be changed is the colour of the beaker.   (1)
3   2 marks for an answer that concludes that cress seeds need water for germination because none germinate in dry conditions, 22% in slightly damp conditions and nearly all in wet conditions. 1 mark if the answer is not explained.   (2)
4   by repeating the test (Also accept, by measuring the amount of water.)   (1)
5   pollination   (1)
6   1 mark each for any two from: wind, carried by animals, explosion and by water   (2)
7   To give the new plant room to grow.   (1)
8   a)   Foam because after 30 minutes the water temperature was higher (55°C) than in the beakers insulated with foil and paper.   (1)
    b)   This was not a fair test because the foam was [ten times] thicker than the other two materials (1). It could be made fair by using exactly the same thickness for each material (1).   (2)
9   1 mark for each plausible answer, for example: creating habitats (e.g. ponds), creating nature reserves, reducing pollution, using renewable energy, recycling, reducing deforestation.   (3)
10   Mammals are born live; most reptiles hatch from eggs.   (1)
11   Pollen joins with an egg (1) and creates a seed (1).   (2)
12   Sperm from the male joins with an egg from the female (1 mark for sperm joining egg, 1 mark for male and female).   (2)
13   1 mark for each correct answer: male – stamen and female – carpel   (2)
14   They produce the food for the plant.   (1)
15   Roots absorb water from the soil (1). The water travels from the roots and up the stem (1). Water moves from the stem and into the leaves (1).   (3)
16   temperature   (1)

## Pages 22–23
### Challenge 1
1   a green plant   (1)
2   a)   producer   (1)
    b)   consumer   (1)
3   1 mark for both answers correct:
An animal that kills and eats another animal = Predator; An animal that is hunted and eaten by a predator = Prey   (1)

### Challenge 2
1   Dandelion leaf ➞ Caterpillar ➞ Vole ➞ Hawk (1 mark for the correct order, 1 mark for arrows pointing the correct way)   (2)
2   dandelion leaf   (1)
3   1 mark for each correct answer: vole, hawk   (2)

### Challenge 3
1   1 mark each for any 2 of: wild cat, jackal and goat   (2)
2   1 mark for each correct answer: snake, wild cat, jackal   (3)
3   3 marks for an answer that explains that the owl, the snake and the kite would be most affected because the snake and the owl would have less to eat so numbers would reduce and then the kite would have less to eat.   (3)
4   Various possible answers:
Green plant ➞ goat ➞ lion
Green plant ➞ rabbit ➞ wild cat ➞ lion
Green plant ➞ rabbit ➞ jackal ➞ lion
Green plant ➞ mouse ➞ wild cat ➞ lion
Green plant ➞ goat ➞ jackal ➞ lion
(1 mark for the correct order, 1 mark for arrows pointing the correct way)   (2)

## Pages 24–25
### Challenge 1
1   1 mark for each correct answer: b) tongue and teeth, c) oesophagus, d) stomach, e) small intestine   (4)
2   1 mark for each correct answer: a) canine, b) molars   (2)

### Challenge 2
1   1 mark for each correct answer: To break down food and to absorb water and nutrients into the body.   (2)
2   To break up food into smaller pieces (1) and to help swallow (1).   (2)

### Challenge 3
1   The digestive system breaks down and absorbs the food and water we consume into nutrients (1) which the body can use for energy, repair and other processes (1).   (2)
2   1 mark for each correctly ordered process:
1 – Food enters the body through the mouth.
2 – The teeth and tongue break food into smaller pieces.
3 – Food is transported down the oesophagus into the stomach.
4 – The stomach churns up food and mixes it with enzymes.
5 – The intestines break food down and absorb water and nutrients.   (4)

## Pages 26–27
### Challenge 1
1   skull   (1)
2   1 mark for each correct answer: supporting the body, protecting organs, supporting movement   (3)
3   1 mark for each correct answer: a) Skull, b) Ribs, c) Spine, d) Pelvis, e) Kneecap   (5)

### Challenge 2
1   1 mark for each correct answer: a) Ribs/Ribcage, b) Pelvis, c) Spine   (3)
2   1 mark for each correct answer: Muscles are attached to the bones by tendons. They work in pairs to help the body move. When one muscle contracts the other one relaxes.   (4)

# Answers

**3**   Award 1 mark for any animal without a skeleton,
e.g. jellyfish, octopus, worm.                                    (1)

## Challenge 3
**1**   To kick the ball the quadriceps and hamstrings work
as a pair (1). When the quadriceps contracts, the
hamstrings relax (1), pulling the foot forward towards
the ball to kick it (1).                                           (3)
**2**   If the skeleton did not have joints, the body would
not be able to bend (1) or move (1).                              (2)

## Pages 28–29
## Challenge 1
**1**   circulatory system                                        (1)
**2**   True                                                      (1)
**3**   1 mark for each correct answer: a – Valve,
b – Atrium, c – Ventricle                                         (3)

## Challenge 2
**1**   **a)**   blood vessels                                    (1)
         **b)**   1 mark for each correct answer: veins, arteries
              and capillaries                                     (3)
**2**   the lungs                                                 (1)
**3**   to stop blood flowing backwards                           (1)

## Challenge 3
**1**   **a)**   By finding their pulse and counting how many
              times their heart beats in a minute.               (1)
         **b)**   It is likely that their heart rates will increase (1)
              because when we are active, our bodies use
              more energy and nutrients and produce
              more waste (1), so the heart needs to beat
              faster (1).                                         (3)
**2**   Any decreasing line on the graph that starts at
180 bpm and levels off at 60 bpm. 1 mark for
decreasing line and 1 mark if it stops decreasing
and levels off at 60 bpm.                                         (2)

## Pages 30–31
## Challenge 1
**1**   1 mark for each correct answer: exercise,
a balanced diet                                                  (2)
**2**   1 mark for each correct answer:

| Food | What it provides for the body |
| --- | --- |
| Berries | **Vitamins and minerals for healthy cells** |
| Butter | Fats for energy |
| Fish | Protein for growth and repair |

                                                                  (3)
**3**   No, bread and butter will not provide all the nutrients
his body needs (1). He needs a variety
of food types to have a balanced diet (1).                        (2)

## Challenge 2
**1**   **a)**   1 mark each for any two of: be active/exercise;
              avoid harmful substances like drugs, cigarettes
              and alcohol; drink plenty of water                  (2)
         **b)**   vitamins and minerals                           (1)
         **c)**   They help keep our cells/bodies healthy.        (1)

**2**   **a)**   Yes                                              (1)
         **b)**   1 mark each for any two of: keep his heart and
              lungs strong and healthy; improve coordination;
              improve muscle strength; use up energy from
              food                                                (2)

## Challenge 3
**1**   Adult B – Because they exercise regularly, don't
smoke and eat a balanced diet.                                    (2)
**2**   Adult D – Because they smoke cigarettes and they
don't exercise or eat a balanced diet.                            (2)
**3**   To stop smoking because it is bad for their health.
It is bad for their heart and lungs, and it can block
arteries and cause heart attacks and even cancer.                (3)

## Pages 32–33
## Challenge 1
**1**   False                                                     (1)
**2**   1 mark for each correct answer: Hair colour and
How tall they are                                                 (2)
**3**   Adaptations                                               (1)

## Challenge 2
**1**   1 mark for either of the following: Humans can adapt
to any environment by changing the clothes they
wear and/or the type of houses they live in. Humans
are also omnivores and can eat almost anything.                  (1)
**2**   thick transparent fur for camouflage and warmth; a
thick layer of fat for warmth; webbed feet for walking
on ice and swimming; black skin for absorbing heat
from the Sun. 1 mark for the adaptation plus an extra
mark for the explanation.                                         (2)
**3**   One mark for each correct answer: webbed feet and
waterproof feathers.                                             (2)

## Challenge 3
**1**   People might think she looks like her sister because
they have each inherited some similar characteristics,
but they cannot be identical.                                     (2)
**2**   Yes, physical characteristics, like the shape of a nose,
can be passed on/inherited for many generations.                (2)
**3**   Waterlilies live in water and therefore do not need
to minimise water loss from their leaves (1) whereas
cacti live in hot, dry environments and need to
minimise their water loss and have adapted to have
small needle-like leaves.                                         (2)

## Pages 34–35
## Challenge 1
**1**   Evolution                                                 (1)
**2**   True                                                      (1)
**3**   Tommy                                                     (1)
**4**   Fossils                                                   (1)

## Challenge 2
**1**   **a)**   Evolution is the theory of how living things have
              changed and adapted (1) over long periods of
              time (1).                                           (2)
         **b)**   Living things evolve because of changes to their
              environment (1) which mean that they need
              to evolve and change themselves in order to
              survive (1).                                        (2)

## Challenge 3
1  a)  1 mark for each physical similarity, e.g. feathers, wings, same shaped legs, similar shaped head, beaks.  (2)
   b)  1 mark for any physical difference, e.g. the archaeopteryx has a longer neck and a longer tail.  (1)
   c)  It could be concluded that the archaeopteryx is an ancestor of modern birds or that modern birds might / could have evolved from dinosaurs.  (1)

## Pages 36–37
### Challenge 1
1  1 mark for all correct: a) liquid, b) gas, c) solid  (1)
2  melting  (1)

### Challenge 2
1  For 2 marks, the explanation should make reference to the water held by the wet washing evaporating in the warm, dry air. 1 mark for 'water evaporates'.  (2)
2  1 mark for each correct answer: oil, oxygen.  (2)

### Challenge 3
1  1 mark for 2 labels correct, 2 marks for all labels correct.

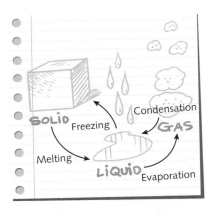

(2)
2  2 marks for an explanation that when warm water vapour in the air (a gas) hits the colder surface of the window it condenses back to liquid water, forming condensation. 1 mark for an acknowledgement that water vapour cools and condenses when it hits the window.  (2)
3  Various answers but must include: measuring the starting amount of water before freezing; measuring the final amount of water after melting; reference to the equipment (e.g. measuring container and freezer).  (3)

## Pages 38–39
### Challenge 1
1  precipitation  (1)
2  False  (1)
3  True  (1)

### Challenge 2
1  1 mark for one correctly matched, 2 marks for all three: Precipitation = When the clouds can no longer hold the water, it falls to the ground; Condensation = As water vapour rises it cools and starts to form clouds; Evaporation = As water is heated, water vapour rises from its surface.  (2)

2  The water from the puddle evaporates into water vapour.  (1)

## Challenge 3
1  1 mark for a correctly labelled diagram and 1 further mark for an explanation of precipitation, evaporation and condensation (see Challenge 2, answer 1) and an additional mark for an acknowledgement that this process is cyclical.  (3)
2  1 mark for an answer which states that most water evaporates at 25°C. 2 marks for an answer which makes a comparison, e.g. the warmer the temperature, the greater the amount of evaporation per hour (or the faster the evaporation).  (2)

## Pages 40–43
### Progress Test 2
1  a green plant  (1)
2  any animal that hunts and eats other animals, e.g. fox, owl, hawk  (1)
3  1 mark for each correct answer: waxy skin, long deep roots, small needle-like leaves  (3)
4  Natural selection is when the living things that are best adapted to their environment survive and reproduce (1) while things that are less adapted fail to survive (1).  (2)
5  Many large predators like lions eat lots of meat. They need more sharp teeth to kill their prey and tear and rip the meat (1) whereas humans eat a variety of foods and need lots of different teeth for different types of food (1).  (2)
6  1 mark for each correctly matched answer: Canine = Tear and rip food; Molar = Crush and grind food; Incisor = Cut and slice food  (3)
7  The bones of the skeleton are held together at the joints by ligaments.  (1)
8  The bones have joints that are held together by ligaments (1) which allow the bones to move (1). Muscles are attached to the bones and work in pairs to make the bones move by contracting and relaxing (1).  (3)
9  1 mark for each correct answer: heart, blood vessels and blood  (3)
10  An ancestor is a person or living thing that lived a long time ago and is related to somebody or something that lived more recently.  (1)
11  a)  the digestive system  (1)
    b)  To break down and digest food into nutrients that the body can use.  (1)
12  1 mark for a correct material in each state, e.g.: Solid – wood, brick, iron, copper, concrete, etc. Liquid – water, oil, fruit juice, etc. Gas – oxygen, carbon dioxide, etc.  (3)
13  a)  Liquid (e.g. water) is heated and turns into vapour (e.g. water vapour) – a gas.  (1)
    b)  Any plausible answer, e.g. drying washing, helps puddles dry, dries the grass, helps to get salt from seawater, helps separate solids dissolved in water.  (1)

# Answers

**14 a)** riding her bike and walking her dog (1)
**b)** 1 mark each for any two from: keep her heart and lungs strong and healthy; use the energy from her food; improve coordination; increase muscle strength (2)
**15** 1 mark for each correct answer: Liquid to solid – freezing, solid to liquid – melting, liquid to gas – evaporating, gas to liquid – condensing (4)
**16** 1 mark for each correct answer: liquids, gases (2)

## Pages 44–45
### Challenge 1
**1** hardness, strength (1)
**2** True (1)
**3** heat (1)

### Challenge 2
**1** 2 marks for a correctly labelled picture:

Insulator

Conductor

(2)
**2** Transparent means that a material is colourless and most of the light that hits it can pass through. Opaque means light cannot pass through the material. (1)

### Challenge 3
**1 a)** 1 mark for both labels correct: spoon – insoluble, sugar – soluble (1)
**b)** The answer must acknowledge that it is important that the spoon is insoluble to avoid it dissolving in the hot drink, and that the sugar is soluble so that it dissolves into the drink. (1)
**2 a)** insulator (1)
**b)** The answer must acknowledge that the bubble wrap proved to be the best insulator and cotton wool was the worst. (1)

## Pages 46–47
### Challenge 1
**1** filtering (1)
**2** True (1)
**3** Answer must acknowledge that they contain holes that allow smaller things to pass through but will not allow anything larger than the holes to pass. (1)

### Challenge 2
**1 a)** it dissolves (1)
**b)** salt solution (1)
**2** The answer should acknowledge that soil passes through the holes in the sieve but stones remain in the sieve. (1)

### Challenge 3
**1** 2 marks for an answer acknowledging that the water evaporates leaving the salt behind. 1 mark for just 'evaporation'. (2)
**2 a)** water (1)
**b)** sand (1)

**3** 2 marks for an answer acknowledging that they needed to be able to condense the evaporated water (i.e. cool it) to turn it back to liquid water. 1 mark for just 'condensation' or 'condense it'. (2)

## Pages 48–49
### Challenge 1
**1** iron (1)
**2** False (1)
**3** permanent (1)

### Challenge 2
**1** 1 mark for each correct answer: cooking an egg, burning wood (2)
**2** The answer must acknowledge that irreversible change can make sure mixed ingredients change into something that tastes better/different. (1)

### Challenge 3
**1** 1 mark for each point: the bicarbonate of soda reacts with the vinegar; the reaction causes fizzing/frothing. (2)
**2** They are wearing safety googles to protect their eyes. (1)

## Pages 50–51
### Challenge 1
**1** metamorphic (1)
**2** 1 mark for each correct answer: Sedimentary – Lots of small rocks compressed over time; Igneous – When magma cools; Metamorphic – Through heat and compression (3)
**3** 1 mark for each correct answer: Water, Organic material, Air and rock particles (4)

### Challenge 2
**1 a)** Rocks B and C (1)
**b)** Rock D (1)
**c)** Rock C because it is soft and permeable. (2)
**d)** Rock A because it is smooth and grey, hard and impermeable. (2)

### Challenge 3
**1 a)** a fossil (1)
**b)** sedimentary (1)
**c)** A long time/millions of years ago, a plant or animal died. It sank to the ground in a watery environment and got covered in layers of sand, mud and stones. Over time, these layers were compressed and formed rock. Eventually, a cast or print of the plant or animal was left in the rock. (4)
**2** The soil changes as she digs because the type of rock particles in the soil changes. The heavier, stickier soil contains more clay than the top layer of soil. (2)

## Pages 52–53
### Challenge 1
**1** Sphere (1)
**2** False (1)

**3** 1 mark for each correct answer:
  **a)** Earth   **b)** Moon   **c)** Sun   (3)

## Challenge 2

**1** 1 mark for each correct answer: It takes approximately **28 (accept any value between 27 and 29 days)** days for the Moon to orbit the **Earth** and approximately 365 days for the Earth to orbit the **Sun**.   (3)

**2 a)** Eight – Mercury, Venus, Earth, Mars, Jupiter, Saturn, Uranus and Neptune.   (2)
  **b)** move around the Sun in a roughly elliptical path   (1)
  **c)** the gravity/gravitational pull from the Sun   (1)

**3** The Moon is a roughly spherical celestial body that orbits the Earth.   (2)

## Challenge 3

**1** Simon is correct (1) because Mercury is closer to the Sun and will orbit the Sun faster, has less distance to travel and will orbit the Sun faster (1).   (2)

**2** 1 mark for each correct answer: The Earth orbits the Sun (1) and is continuously rotating (1).   (2)

**3** Venus is reflecting the light from the Sun (1) just like the Moon does (1).   (2)

## Pages 54–55
## Challenge 1
**1**

Night   Day
  (1)

**2** The Earth rotating around its axis   (1)
**3** 24 hours   (1)

## Challenge 2

**1** The Earth has rotated and the places that are experiencing night time are not facing the Sun and cannot receive its warmth and light.   (2)
**2** The Earth's axis is slightly tilted   (1)
**3** A sundial or the position of the Sun in the sky.   (1)

## Challenge 3

**1** midday   (1)
**2** C – shadows are shortest at midday or 1 mark for correct answer, extra mark for simple explanation   (2)
**3 a)** 1 mark for any position along the dotted line on the east side of the diagram labelled morning.   (1)
  **b)** 1 mark for any position along the dotted line on the west side of the diagram labelled evening.   (1)

## Pages 56–57
## Challenge 1
**1** 1 mark for each correct answer: Light is a form of energy, Light is needed to be able to see, and Light can be reflected   (3)

**2** Natural: Sun, Fire, Firefly
  Artificial: Torch, Glow stick, Mobile phone   (1)
**3** a smooth silver coin   (1)

## Challenge 2

**1** No, darkness is not a type of light, it is the absence of light.   (2)
**2** He needs to protect his eyes because the light from the Sun is very powerful and can damage them. He can protect his eyes by wearing sunglasses and a sunhat, staying in the shade and not looking directly at the Sun.   (2)
**3** it is absorbed   (1)

## Challenge 3

**1 a)** the Moon   (1)
  **b)** The Moon may appear to be a light source because it looks like it is shining whereas it is actually reflecting the light from the Sun.   (2)
  **c)** Any one natural source of light e.g. lightning, stars, luminescent plants or animals such as certain jellyfish or mushrooms.   (1)

**2 a)** They find it difficult to see because there is less light (1) which means less light will be reflecting off the road signs and into their eyes, making them more difficult to see (1).   (2)
  **b)** A torch, glow stick or any other portable light source.   (1)
  **c)** Reflective materials work by reflecting almost all the light from a source (1). When a car's headlights shine onto the jackets, the light is reflected back to the driver, making it easier for Jamie and Freddy to be seen (1).   (2)

## Pages 58–59
## Challenge 1
**1** 1 mark for each correct answer: Light travels **quickly** in **straight** lines, and it **cannot** bend around corners.   (3)
**2** Accept a line that that is straight from the candle into the eye with the arrow pointing in the direction of the eye.   (2)
**3** mirror   (1)

## Challenge 2

**1** The light from the Sun is shining on the dog. It reflects off the dog and into Millie's eyes. Her eyes send a signal to the brain, and the brain tells her she is seeing her dog.   (3)
**2 a)** No   (1)
  **b)** Unlike sound, light can travel through a **vacuum**.   (1)
  **c)** When the light from the Sun travels to the Earth, through the vacuum of space.   (2)

## Challenge 3

**1 a)** He could see her reflection in the mirror.   (1)
  **b)** The light from the lamp fell on his mum, and was reflected off his mum and onto the mirror where it was reflected into Oliver's eyes.   (2)

# Answers

c) 1 mark awarded for each correct arrow: 1 straight arrow from the light to Oliver. 1 straight arrow from Oliver to the mirror and 1 straight arrow from the mirror to Mum. (3)

**Pages 60–61**
**Challenge 1**
1  3 marks for all three correctly matched: Transparent = Allows all or most light to pass through; Translucent = Allows some light to pass through; Opaque = Does not allow any light to pass through. (3)
2  3 marks for all three correctly matched: 1 = b, 2 = c and 3 = a (3)
3  When an object is closer to a source of **light**, its **shadow** will be **bigger**. (1)

**Challenge 2**
1  a) opaque (1)
   b) Light travels in straight lines and cannot bend around objects. (1)
   c) Accept any diagram showing the puppet between the torch and the screen with the light from the torch shining on the puppet. (2)
   d) The shadow is formed because the puppet is opaque and blocks the light from the torch. The light does not reach the screen and a shadow is formed. (1)

**Challenge 3**
1  a) No (1)
   b) 1 mark for each correct answer: the position of the screen and torch, and the object. (2)
   c) 11 – (Accept any number between 10–12) (1)
   d) The size of a shadow decreases as the distance between the light source and the object increases. (2)

**Pages 62–65**
**Progress Test 3**
1  They can make/produce their own food. (1)
2  After the stomach, food moves into the intestines where it is broken down into nutrients and absorbed into the body. (2)
3  The circulatory system transports the nutrients (1) around the body. It also transports oxygen (1) and water (1). (3)
4  the skull (1)
5  permeable (1)
6  fossils (1)
7  a) No (1)
   b) The Moon looks bright because it reflects the light from the Sun. (2)
   c) The Moon is spherical like a ball. It appears to change shape because, as the Earth orbits the Sun and the Earth, we see different amounts of the Moon lit up by the Sun meaning only part of the Moon can be seen. (2)

8  a)

mirror set at 45° angle
object
box
eye
mirror set at 45° angle (2)
   b) mirrors (1)
   c) reflection (1)
9  irreversible (or non-reversible) (1)
10 a) They would pour the dirty water into the filter paper (1). Cleaner water will pass through the filter into the glass flask, while sand and gravel will stay on the filter paper (1). (2)
   b) The sand and gravel could be separated with a sieve (1). The sand should fall through the sieve but the larger gravel will stay in the sieve (1). (2)
11 1 mark for each correct answer. Example answers: **Irreversible:** cooking an egg, baking a cake, baking bread (1); **Reversible:** melting chocolate, melting butter (1) (2)
12 No, it is never safe to look directly at the Sun because the light from the Sun is very powerful and can damage the eye. (2)
13 1 mark for each correct answer. Example answers: **Thermal insulator:** wood, plastic, fabric (1); **Thermal conductor:** metal (2)
14 1 mark for an acknowledgement that they react with each other. 1 mark for fizzing/bubbling/frothing. (2)
15 To make sure there are no errors or anything affecting the results. (1)
16 precipitation (1)
17 The Sun appears to move across the sky because the Earth is rotating (1). During the day, the Earth continues to rotate, making it seem that the Sun is travelling across the sky. At night time, the Sun is shining on the far side of the Earth (1). (2)
18 A shadow is formed when an opaque object blocks light from a source. (2)

**Pages 66–67**
**Challenge 1**
1  1 mark for each correct answer: Forces are pushes and pulls, which are measured in **Newtons**. When forces are **unbalanced**, they can make objects move. (2)
2  Water resistance (1)
3  True (1)

**Challenge 2**
1  friction (1)
2  Ice does not create a lot of friction and cars might slip and slide. The rock salt will provide more friction so that the tyres can grip the road. (2)
3  streamlined (1)

# Answers

## Challenge 3

1. 
   a) The force comes from the man (1). The move is a push (1). (2)
   b) Air resistance and friction are acting on the man and his bike. They are acting in the opposite direction to the bike's movement and will be slowing it down. (3)
   c) The force of the push on the pedals is stronger than the forces acting against the bike. The forces are unbalanced, which makes the bike continue to move. (2)
   d) When the man stops pedalling, the forces become balanced, which makes the bike stop. (1)
   e) The bikes need different tyres because they travel on different surfaces and are used to go at different speeds (1). The smooth, thin tyres of the racing bike will create less friction with the road and allow the bike to move faster and more easily when the road is dry (1). The wide, rough tyres of the mountain bike will create more friction and will give the bike more grip which will help it go up and down mountains more easily and safely (1). (3)
   f) The racing bike might be more streamlined to reduce air resistance and allow the bike to move more easily through the air. (Accept any reasonable suggestion.) (1)

## Pages 68–69
### Challenge 1
1. They can act from a distance (1)
2. True (1)
3. 1 mark for each correct answer: paper clip and magnet (2)

### Challenge 2
1. 1 mark for each correct answer: north and south poles (2)
2. (1)

   N S   N S

3. Gravity pulls the ball back to the ground. (2)

### Challenge 3
1. 
   a) compass (1)
   b) (2)

2. Gravity acts equally all around the Earth, pulling objects and people towards its centre. (2)

3. Accept any two: Gravity pulls objects towards the centre of the Earth; Gravity from the Earth keeps the Moon in orbit; Gravity from the Sun holds the planets of the solar system in orbit. (2)

## Pages 70–71
### Challenge 1
1. 1 mark for each correct answer:
   Lever = A pivot and a long beam
   Gear = Wheels with teeth around the edge
   Pulley = A rope running over a wheel (3)
2. Pulley (1)

### Challenge 2
1. 
   a) pulley (1)
   b) It changes the direction of the force needed. It is easier to pull down using gravity to help than it is to lift, pulling upwards, against gravity. (2)
   c) Mandy has made a lever. The lever increases the effect of the push force that she applies to it and makes it easier to move the rock. (3)

### Challenge 3
1. 
   a) 1 mark for each correct answer: B: Anticlockwise C: Clockwise (2)
   b) Gear C (1)
   c) Gear A (1)
   d) 1 mark for each correct answer: Accept any example where a gear is used, e.g. bicycles, cars, clocks. (2)

## Pages 72–73
### Challenge 1
1. **Sound** is made when an **object or material vibrates**. The vibrations travel through a **medium** to the **eardrum** and sound is heard. (5)
2. 1 mark for each correct answer: the air, a window and water. (3)
3. True (1)

### Challenge 2
1. When the bell is shaken, the clapper hits the bell causing the bell to vibrate and make a sound. (2)
2. air (1)
3. The children may not have heard the bell because sound gets quieter/fainter the further it travels. The children might be too far away to hear the bell clearly. (2)

### Challenge 3
1. Hitting the railings makes them vibrate (1), the vibrations travel from the railings to Luiz's ears (1), the eardrum sends a signal to the brain and sound is heard (1). (3)
2. 1 mark for each correct answer: the railings and the air. (2)
3. Sound travels faster through solids and liquids than other mediums (1). The railings are solid so the sound travels through the railings faster than it does through the air so he can hear the sound through the railings and then the sound through the air (1). (2)

# Answers

**4** Katie is correct because as sound travels it gets fainter. As the vibrations travel, they lose energy, and the vibrations get smaller/weaker. (2)

**Pages 74–75**
**Challenge 1**
**1** How loud or quiet a sound is. (1)
**2** 1 mark for each correct answer:
   **a)** fainter **b)** more/louder **c)** pitch (3)
**3** 1 mark for each correct answer: a small bird, a small bell, an alarm (3)

**Challenge 2**
**1** Toby's – hitting the bars harder provides more energy and makes bigger vibrations which make a louder sound. (2)
**2** High-pitched sounds – the shorter bars vibrate faster and make a higher-pitched sound. (2)
**3** The pitch will start high, but as the bars get bigger, the pitch will get lower and lower (1). This happens because the bars are getting bigger (1) which means that they will vibrate more slowly and create a lower pitch (1). (3)

**Challenge 3**
**1** No, the thicker bands will make a lower-pitched sound because they vibrate more slowly. (3)
**2** She has made sure that all the bands are the same length. (1)
**2** **a)** Sound wave A (1)
   **b)** Accept any sound wave with a greater frequency than wave B but smaller than wave A

(1)

**Pages 76–77**
**Challenge 1**
**1** 1 mark for each correct answer:
Mains electricity: washing machine, television, freezer/Battery: torch, mobile phone (5)
**2** True (1)
**3** energy (1)

**Challenge 2**
**1** 1 mark for each correct label.

(3)

**2** 1 mark for correctly drawn symbol.

(1)

**Challenge 3**
**1** **a)**

(1)

   **b)** Because the circuit is complete (electricity can flow round the circuit) when the switch is on. (1)
**2** **a)** C (1)
   **b)** The explanation should acknowledge that the circuit is not complete in the other pictures. (1)

**Pages 78–79**
**Challenge 1**
**1** a switch (1)
**2** 1 mark for each correct answer: paper clip, nail (2)
**3** an insulator (1)

**Challenge 2**
**1** Plastic is an insulator and protects against electric shocks (1). Metal is a conductor and helps electricity to flow from the mains electricity supply to appliances (1). (2)
**2** **a)** 1 mark for correctly drawn open switch (off).

   **b)** 1 mark for correctly drawn closed switch (on). (2)

**Challenge 3**
**1** **a)** will not sound (1)
   **b)** will sound (1)
   **c)** will not sound (1)
**2** The explanation should include:
When closed (or 'on'), the switch conducts electricity, making the circuit (1). When open (or 'off') the switch breaks the circuit because electricity cannot flow (1). (2)

**Pages 80–81**
**Challenge 1**
**1** Provides energy (electricity) to the circuit. (1)
**2** 1 mark for a correctly drawn battery symbol.

(1)

**3** 1 mark for each correct answer: more batteries and a higher-powered battery (2)

**Challenge 2**
**1** 1 mark for each of: battery, motor, buzzer, switch, wires (4)

**2** 2 marks for a correctly drawn circuit diagram as below. 1 mark if no more than one component is missing and the circuit is complete. (2)

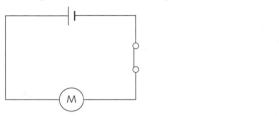

**Challenge 3**

**1 a)** 2 marks for a correctly drawn circuit diagram as below. 1 mark if no more than one component is missing and the circuit is complete. (2)

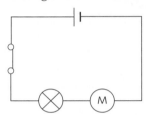

**b)** Circuit as above but with at least one additional battery. (1)

**2** Too much power could damage or break any components in the circuit. (1)

**Pages 82–84**

**Progress Test 4**

**1** Igneous rock is formed when molten rock, magma or lava cools (1), whereas metamorphic rock is formed when other types of rock are heated and put under high pressure (1). (2)

**2 a)** The kittens are different because they have inherited different characteristics from each parent (1). It is called variation (1). (2)

**b)** The male cat might have been ginger because some of the kittens were ginger or had ginger patches. (1)

**3 a)** A push force. The force comes from the air that is pumped into the rocket from the plunger. (2)

**b)** There is no longer a force acting against gravity. The forces become unbalanced and gravity pulls the rocket back to the Earth. (2)

**4 a)** The light travels from the cinema screen into their eyes. Their eyes send a signal to their brains, and their brains interpret what they are seeing. (2)

**b)** The speakers vibrate and make a sound wave. The sound wave makes the air vibrate and these vibrations reach the eardrum. (2)

**5** Tightening the strings will cause them to make a higher-pitched sound. (1)

**6 a)** A conductor allows electricity to pass through it (1), and an insulator prevents electricity from passing through (1). (2)

**b)** wire [electrical wire/cable], power lines, plug (metal pins), lightning conductor (1)

**c)** plastic around a wire/cable, plastic coating on a plug (1)

**7** Different-sized gears make the hands of the watch move at different speeds (1) Bigger gears with more teeth turn more slowly than smaller gears with fewer teeth (1) (2)

**8 a)** 1 mark each for: bulb, buzzer (2)

**b)** The switch makes/completes the circuit (1) when it is closed (or 'on'), and it can break the circuit (1) when it is open (or 'off'). Award 1 mark for any acknowledgement that the switch controls the other components by controlling the flow of electricity that they need to work. (2)

**9** A vertebrate has a backbone but an invertebrate does not. (1)

**10** Water vapour cools down (1), turns back to liquid and forms clouds or droplets (1). (2)

**11** Soluble materials will dissolve [in water] (1). Insoluble materials will not dissolve [in water] (1) (2)

**12** igneous rock (1)

# Progress Test Charts

## Progress Test 1

| Q | Topic | ✓ or ✗ | See Page |
|---|---|---|---|
| 1 | Asking Scientific Questions and Collecting Data | | 4 |
| 2 | Asking Scientific Questions and Collecting Data | | 4 |
| 3 | Making Conclusions and Using Evidence | | 6 |
| 4 | Asking Scientific Questions and Collecting Data | | 4 |
| 5 | Reproduction | | 14 |
| 6 | Reproduction | | 14 |
| 7 | Reproduction | | 14 |
| 8 | Making Conclusions and Using Evidence | | 6 |
| 9 | Changing Environments | | 16 |
| 10 | Life Cycles | | 12 |
| 11 | Reproduction | | 14 |
| 12 | Reproduction | | 14 |
| 13 | Reproduction | | 14 |
| 14 | Parts of Plants | | 10 |
| 15 | Parts of Plants | | 10 |
| 16 | Asking Scientific Questions and Collecting Data | | 4 |

## Progress Test 2

| Q | Topic | ✓ or ✗ | See Page |
|---|---|---|---|
| 1 | Food Chains | | 22 |
| 2 | Food Chains | | 22 |
| 3 | Adaptation and Variation | | 32 |
| 4 | Adaptation and Variation | | 32 |
| 5 | Adaptation and Variation | | 32 |
| 6 | Digestion | | 24 |
| 7 | Skeleton and Muscles | | 26 |
| 8 | Skeleton and Muscles | | 26 |
| 9 | Heart and Blood Vessels | | 28 |
| 10 | Evidence for Evolution | | 34 |
| 11 | Digestion | | 24 |
| 12 | Solids, Liquids and Gases | | 36 |
| 13 | Solids, Liquids and Gases | | 36 |
| 14 | Healthy Living | | 30 |
| 15 | Solids, Liquids and Gases | | 36 |
| 16 | Solids, Liquids and Gases | | 36 |

## Progress Test 3

| Q | Topic | ✓ or ✗ | See Page |
|---|---|---|---|
| 1 | Food Chains | | 22 |
| 2 | Digestion | | 24 |
| 3 | Heart and Blood Vessels | | 28 |
| 4 | Skeleton and Muscles | | 26 |
| 5 | Rocks and Soil | | 50 |
| 6 | Rocks and Soil | | 50 |
| 7 | The Solar System | | 52 |
| 8 | How Light Travels | | 58 |
| 9 | Irreversible Changes | | 48 |
| 10 | Reversible Changes | | 46 |
| 11 | Reversible Changes / Irreversible Changes | | 46, 48 |
| 12 | Light and Dark | | 56 |
| 13 | Properties and Uses of Materials | | 44 |
| 14 | Irreversible Changes | | 48 |
| 15 | Asking Scientific Questions and Collecting Data | | 4 |
| 16 | The Water Cycle | | 38 |
| 17 | Day and Night | | 54 |
| 18 | Shadows | | 60 |

## Progress Test 4

| Q | Topic | ✓ or ✗ | See Page |
|---|---|---|---|
| 1 | Rocks and Soil | | 50 |
| 2 | Adaptation and Variation | | 32 |
| 3 | Contact Forces / Magnets and Gravity | | 66, 68 |
| 4 | How Light Travels / Making Sounds | | 58, 72 |
| 5 | Pitch and Volume | | 74 |
| 6 | Properties and Uses of Materials | | 44 |
| 7 | Levers, Pulleys and Gears | | 70 |
| 8 | Making Circuits / Breaking Circuits / Cells in Circuits | | 76, 78, 80 |
| 9 | Grouping Living Things | | 8 |
| 10 | The Water Cycle | | 38 |
| 11 | Properties and Uses of Materials | | 44 |
| 12 | Rocks and Soil | | 50 |

What am I doing well in? _____

_____

What do I need to improve? _____

_____

**15** What are the processes known as during the following changes of state?

Liquid to solid: _____

Solid to liquid: _____

Liquid to gas: _____

Gas to liquid: _____

**16** Materials in which two states of matter change shape if they are moved from one shape of container to another?

_____

Marks........ /36

# Properties and Uses of Materials

## Challenge 1

1 What property does concrete have that makes it good for building?

_____

1 mark

2 **True** or **false**? Water can conduct electricity.

_____

1 mark

3 Complete the sentence: A thermal conductor allows
_____ to travel through it.

1 mark

Marks.........../3

## Challenge 2

1 Look at the picture of an electrical wire. Label the materials used, using the words insulator and conductor.

2 marks

2 What is the difference between the terms transparent and opaque?

_____

_____

1 mark

Marks.........../3

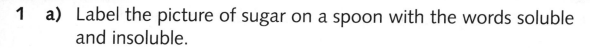

# Properties and Uses of Materials

**Challenge 3**

**1 a)** Label the picture of sugar on a spoon with the words soluble and insoluble.

1 mark

**b)** Explain how the terms soluble and insoluble are both important when stirring sugar into a hot drink.

_____

_____

1 mark

**2** A class has three identical containers of warm water, all with the same amount of water at the same temperature. One is wrapped in foil, one is wrapped in cotton wool and one is wrapped in bubble wrap.

Glass beaker containing water, wrapped in foil

Glass beaker containing water, wrapped in cotton wool

Glass beaker containing water, wrapped in bubble wrap

**a)** The class is measuring which material keeps the water warmest. This means they are measuring which is the best

_____.

1 mark

**b)** After 30 minutes, the water in the container wrapped in cotton wool is the coolest, and the water in the container wrapped in bubble wrap is the warmest. What conclusion can they draw from this?

_____

1 mark

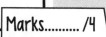
Marks............/4

**Total marks** ............ /10       How am I doing?

# Reversible Changes

## Challenge 1

**1** Which process is usually used to separate fine solids from a liquid?

sieving ☐ filtering ☐

*1 mark*

**2** **True** or **false**? Melting ice is a reversible change.

_____

*1 mark*

**3** How does a sieve separate materials?

_____

_____

*1 mark*

Marks.........../3

## Challenge 2

**1 a)** What happens to salt when it is mixed with water?

_____

*1 mark*

**b)** What do we call the mixture of water and salt?

_____

*1 mark*

**3** Why would a sieve be used to separate stones from dry sand?

_____

_____

*1 mark*

Marks.........../3

# Reversible Changes

**Challenge 3**

1   The picture below shows salt ponds in a hot climate. Salty sea water flows into the ponds and is then trapped, eventually leaving behind solid salt. The salt is then used in different ways.

Explain how solid salt gets to be left in the salt ponds.

_____

_____

_____

_____

_____

2 marks

2   Sand and water are mixed together. This mixture is then poured through filter paper.

   **a)** What would you expect to pass through the filter paper?

   _____

   1 mark

   **b)** What would you expect to be left on the filter paper?

   _____

   1 mark

3   During an investigation to separate sugar from water using evaporation, the class realise that they have wasted the evaporated water.

Explain what they could have done to collect this water.

_____

_____

2 marks

Marks.......... /6

Total marks ............. /12          How am I doing?

# Irreversible Changes

## Challenge 1

1   Which material can change to rust?

plastic ☐            aluminium ☐            iron ☐

1 mark

2   **True** or **false**? Melting chocolate is an irreversible change.

_____

1 mark

3   If a material is changed irreversibly, it means the change is:

quick ☐            permanent ☐            temporary ☐

1 mark

Marks.........../3

## Challenge 2

1   Tick each irreversible change.

cooking an egg ☐            dissolving salt ☐

burning wood ☐            mixing different stones ☐

bending metal ☐            melting butter ☐

2 marks

2   Explain why irreversible changes can be very useful in cooking.

_____

_____

1 mark

Marks.........../3

# Irreversible Changes

## Challenge 3

**1** The children in the picture below have made a model volcano.

In the top of the volcano they have put baking soda (also known as bicarbonate of soda), and added just a little orange food colouring to represent lava.

They have then added vinegar.

Explain why their volcano appears to be erupting.

_____

_____

_____

2 marks

**2** What safety precaution have the children in the picture taken?

_____

1 mark

Marks.........../3

Total marks ............ /9          How am I doing?

# Rocks and Soil

## Challenge 1

**1** Slate and marble are examples of which type of rock? Tick **one**.

sedimentary ☐     igneous ☐     metamorphic ☐

**2** Match the type of rock to the way that it is formed.

| Sedimentary | | When magma cools |
| --- | --- | --- |
| Igneous | | Through heat and compression |
| Metamorphic | | Lots of small rocks compressed over time |

**3** Circle the **four** things that make up soil.

Water            Plastic            Air

Organic material      Living insects      Rock particles

Marks.......... /8

## Challenge 2

**1** The children in Class 3 are investigating rocks. They completed a table to show what happened when they tried different tests on four different rocks.

| Rock | Appearance | Does a fingernail scratch it? | Will it allow water through? |
| --- | --- | --- | --- |
| A | Smooth, hard and grey | No | No |
| B | Rough with lots of smaller stones inside | No | Yes |
| C | White, soft and grainy | Yes | Yes |
| D | Contains crystals (minerals) | No | No |

**a)** Which **two** rocks are permeable?

_____     _____

**b)** Which rock is most likely to be igneous?

_____

# Rocks and Soil

**c)** The teacher tells them that one of their rocks is chalk. Which rock is this and how do you know?

_____

2 marks

**d)** Slate is a smooth grey or black rock that is hard and often used as a roof tile because it is impermeable. Which rock is most likely to be slate? Why?

_____

2 marks

Marks.......... /6

## Challenge 3

**1** Niamh was helping her Dad to dig the garden when she came across a piece of rock with what looked like the print of an animal on it.

**a)** What was on the rock that Niamh found?

_____

1 mark

**b)** What type of rock is it most likely to have been made in?

_____

1 mark

**c)** Explain how the print of the animal was formed.

_____

_____

_____

4 marks

**2** Niamh is excited to try and find some more and continues to dig. At first, the soil is dry, sandy and easy to dig. As she digs deeper, the soil changes and gets heavier, stickier and harder to dig. Why has the soil changed?

_____

_____

_____

2 marks

Marks.......... /8

Total marks ............ /22          How am I doing?

# The Solar System

## Challenge 1

**1** The Earth, Sun and Moon are all roughly the same shape. Circle the correct shape from the choices below.

Circle          Cylinder          Sphere          Square

*1 mark*

**2** **True** or **false**? The planets move around freely in space and change their order. _____

*1 mark*

**3** Use the words from the box to correctly complete these sentences.

| Earth | Sun | Moon |

**a)** The _____ orbits the Sun.

**b)** The _____ reflects light from the Sun.

**c)** The _____ heats and lights up the Earth.

*3 marks*

Marks.......... /5

## Challenge 2

**1** Complete the sentence below.

It takes approximately _____ days for the Moon to orbit the _____ and approximately 365 days for the Earth to orbit the _____.

*3 marks*

**2** All of the planets in the solar system orbit the Sun.

**a)** How many planets are in the solar system? Name them all.

_____

_____

*2 marks*

**b)** What does the word orbit mean?

_____

*1 mark*

**c)** What keeps the planets in orbit?

_____

*1 mark*

# The Solar System

**3** What is the Moon and how does it move?

_____

_____

2 marks

Marks.......... /9

## Challenge 3

**1** Simon and Fred are discussing the planets. Simon thinks that Mercury will orbit the Sun faster than Neptune, but Fred believes Neptune will be faster. Who do you think is correct and why?

_____

_____

2 marks

**2** The Earth is constantly moving in space. Explain **two** ways in which the Earth is moving.

_____

_____

2 marks

**3** The planet Venus can sometimes be seen in the night sky. It looks like it is shining, but Venus does not produce light. Use your knowledge of the Moon to explain what might be happening.

_____

_____

2 marks

Marks.......... /6

**Total marks** ............. /20        How am I doing?

# Day and Night

## Challenge 1

1   On the diagram below, label which side of the Earth is in day time and which side is in night time.

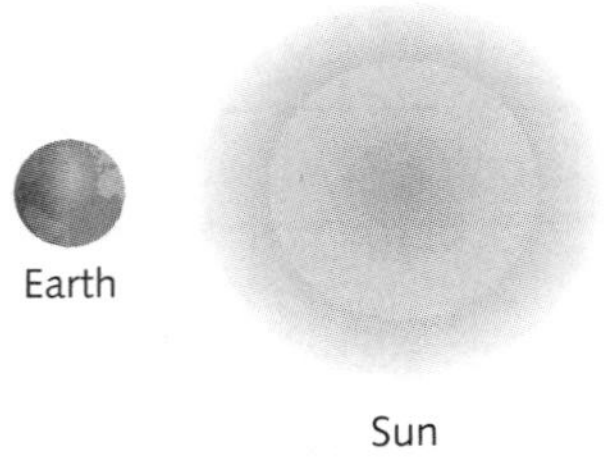

Earth

Sun

☐ 1 mark

2   Which of the following movements causes day and night? Tick **one**.

The Earth orbiting the Sun ☐

The Sun moving away from the Earth ☐

The Earth rotating around its axis ☐

The Moon orbiting the Earth ☐

☐ 1 mark

3   Approximately how long does it take the Earth to make one full rotation? Circle the correct answer.

12 Hours        365 Days        28 Days        24 Hours

☐ 1 mark

Marks.........../3

## Challenge 2

1   At night time, it is darker and cooler than during the day. What happens that causes these changes?

_____

_____

☐ 2 marks

2   The Earth always takes the same amount of time to make a full rotation, but in summer the daylight time is longer and the night time is shorter.

Which **one** of the following is responsible for the difference?

The Earth rotates more slowly in summer. ☐

The Earth's axis is slightly tilted. ☐

The Sun moves more slowly across the sky in summer. ☐

☐ 1 mark

**3** Name an instrument or technique people used to have, before watches, to help them to tell the time.

_____

1 mark

Marks.......... /4

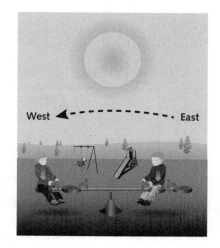

West ◄------------- East

**1** What time of day is shown in the diagram above?

_____

1 mark

**2** The length of the shadow made by the slide was measured at three different times in the day. The measurements were as follows:

Shadow A: 240 cm        Shadow B: 320 cm        Shadow C: 120 cm

Which of these shadows is most likely to have been formed when the Sun was in the position shown in the diagram above? Explain your answer.

_____

2 marks

**3** On the dotted line on the diagram above, mark and label where the Sun could be at the following times:

**a)** In the morning        **b)** In the evening

2 marks

Marks.......... /5

Total marks ............. /12        How am I doing?

55

# Light and Dark

## Challenge 1

**1** Tick the statements that are **true** about light and dark.

Light is a form of energy. ☐

Light can be reflected. ☐

Light is needed to be able to see. ☐

Light is never dangerous. ☐

*3 marks*

**2** Sort these light sources into natural and artificial sources.

Sun    Torch    Glow stick    Mobile phone    Fire    Firefly

| **Natural** | **Artificial** |
|---|---|
|  |  |

*1 mark*

**3** Which object would reflect the most light? Circle **one**.

A wooden bench     A cotton T-shirt     A smooth silver coin

*1 mark*

Marks.......... /5

## Challenge 2

**1** Laura believes that darkness is a type of light. Is she correct? Can you explain what darkness is?

_____

_____

*2 marks*

**2** Sam wakes up one morning and notices that it is a very bright, sunny day. He decides that he is going to spend the day playing in the garden. Why does Sam need to protect his eyes and how can he do it?

_____

_____

*2 marks*

**3** Some materials reflect more light than others. What happens to any light that hits an opaque object but is not reflected by it?

_____

*1 mark*

Marks.......... /5

# Light and Dark

## Challenge 3

**1**   The children in Class 4 are discussing natural light sources. They make a list which contains: the Sun, a fire, a firefly and the Moon.

    **a)**   Which **one** of the sources on the list is not a source of light?

_____

*1 mark*

    **b)**   Why might the children think that it is a source of light?

_____

_____

*2 marks*

    **c)**   Name another natural light source that could be added to the list.

_____

*1 mark*

**2**   One evening, Jamie and Freddy are walking home from football. They notice that it is harder to read the road signs now that there is no sunlight.

    **a)**   Explain why Jamie and Freddy are finding it difficult to see and read the road signs.

_____

_____

_____

*2 marks*

    **b)**   What could they take with them next time that might help them to see the road signs?

_____

*1 mark*

    **c)**   They also decide to wear special reflective jackets so that drivers can see them more easily. How do the reflective jackets work?

_____

_____

_____

*2 marks*

Marks.......... /9

Total marks ............. /19    How am I doing?

# How Light Travels

## Challenge 1

**1** Circle the underlined correct words to complete the sentence.

Light travels <u>slowly/quickly</u> in <u>straight/wavy</u> lines, and it <u>can/cannot</u> bend around corners.

3 marks

**2** Draw lines to show how the light travels from a candle to the eye. Include arrows to show which way the light is travelling.

2 marks

**3** Which of the following items is useful because it is reflective? Circle **one**.

| computer | mirror | light bulb | spoon |

1 mark

Marks.......... /6

## Challenge 2

**1** Millie is watching her dog play in the garden on a sunny day. Explain how she can see her dog.

_____

_____

_____

3 marks

**2** Last term, Class 4 learnt all about sound and how it travels. This term they are learning about light. They make the prediction that light will need a medium to travel through, just like sound.

**a)** Is their prediction correct? _____

1 mark

**b)** Complete the sentence: Unlike sound, light can travel through a _____.

1 mark

**c)** Give an example of when light travels in this way.

_____

_____

2 marks

Marks.......... /7

# How Light Travels

**Challenge 3**

**1** One morning, Oliver was getting ready for school. He was brushing his teeth and looking in the mirror when his mum walked in behind him and smiled.

**a)** Oliver could see that his mum had come into the bathroom without turning to look. How could he see his mum?

_____

1 mark

**b)** It was dark that morning, so the lights in the bathroom were on. Describe how the light travelled and allowed Oliver to see his mum.

_____

_____

2 marks

**c)** When he had finished brushing his teeth, Oliver pulled a funny face at his mum in the mirror. On the diagram below, draw the path of the light which allowed his mum to see him pull the face.

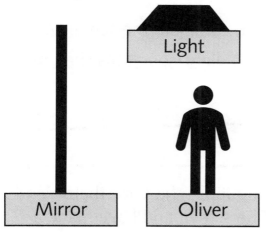

Light

Mirror          Oliver          Mum

3 marks

Marks.......... /6

Total marks ............. /19          How am I doing?

59

# Shadows

## Challenge 1

**1** Match the words to the correct definitions.

| Transparent | Allows some light to pass through. |
| Translucent | Does not allow any light to pass through. |
| Opaque | Allows all or most light to pass through. |

*3 marks*

**2** Draw lines to match the objects to their shadows.

1

2

3

a

b

c

*3 marks*

**3** Circle the correct underlined words to complete the sentence.

When an object is closer to a source of <u>light/sound</u>, its <u>shadow/reflection</u> will be <u>bigger/smaller</u>.

*1 mark*

Marks.........../7

## Challenge 2

**1** Delilah and Mya want to perform a puppet show for their friend Imran. They have a torch and a white screen and have made a selection of puppets which are all the same size.

**a)** For the puppets to make sharp shadows, do they need to be made from translucent, transparent or opaque materials?

_____

*1 mark*

**b)** Mya is worried that the light from the torch will go around the objects and the shadows won't be the same shape as the puppets. Why is this not possible?

_____

_____

*1 mark*

**c)** Draw and label a diagram, on a separate sheet of paper, showing how the torch, puppet and screen need to be positioned to make shadows on the screen.

2 marks

**d)** Why is the shadow formed?

_____

_____

1 mark

Marks.......... /5

## Challenge 3

**1** The children in Class 5 are investigating the relationship between the distance of an object from a light source and the size of its shadow. They use a torch, ruler, cardboard shape and a screen.

The results are shown in the table below.

| Distance of objects from torch (cm) | 5 | 10 | 15 | 20 |
|---|---|---|---|---|
| Height of shadow (cm) | 20 | 17 | 14 | |

**a)** They predicted that the shadow would get bigger as the distance from the light source increased. Was their prediction accurate?

_____

1 mark

**b)** To ensure that this was a fair test, name **two** things that they kept the same.

_____

2 marks

**c)** Use the results provided to predict the size of the shadow when the object is 20 cm from the torch. _____

1 mark

**d)** What conclusion can be drawn from this experiment?

_____

_____

2 marks

Marks.......... /6

**Total marks** .............. /18

How am I doing?

**1** Why are plants known as producers?

_____

*1 mark*

**2** In the digestive system, where does food go after it has been in the stomach and what happens there?

_____

_____

_____

*2 marks*

**3** Once nutrients from food have been absorbed by the digestive system, which system transports them around the body? What else does that system transport?

_____

_____

*3 marks*

**4** The human brain is a vital organ. Which part of the skeleton has the job of protecting the brain?

_____

*1 mark*

**5** Sandy or gravelly soil allows water to pass through it quite easily. What word can be used to describe this feature of the soil?

_____

*1 mark*

**6** Sedimentary rock is made up of sand, small stones, plant and animal remains and mud. What else can sedimentary rock contain which helps us to see how living things have evolved?

_____

*1 mark*

**7** George and Annabelle are talking about the Moon. Annabelle believes that we can see at night because the Moon produces light.

**a)** Is Annabelle correct? _____

*1 mark*

**b)** Why does the Moon look so bright?

_____

*2 marks*

c) George thinks that the Moon is always changing shape. What shape is the Moon and why might George think that its shape changes?

_______________

_______________

_______________

2 marks

8 a) On the diagram below, draw lines to show how the light travels to enable the person using the periscope to see over a fence. Be sure to include arrows to show which way the light is travelling.

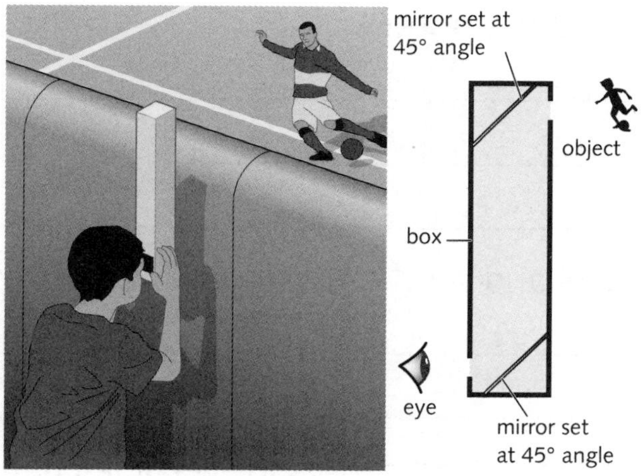

mirror set at
45° angle
object
box
eye
mirror set
at 45° angle

2 marks

b) What objects does the periscope use to make the light change direction?

_______________

1 mark

c) What is it called when light bounces off another object in this way?

_______________

1 mark

9 What sort of change is the process of rusting?

_______________

1 mark

**10** Each child is given a glass flask, a funnel and filter paper as below.

    **a)** Explain how they would use this equipment and what they would see happen when separating sand and gravel from water they have collected from a pond.

_____

_____

_____

    **b)** Explain how the gravel and sand could be separated.

_____

_____

**11** Nisha says that heating some food causes irreversible change, but changes from heating other food are reversible.

Name one type of food that goes through irreversible change when heated, and one type of food that goes through reversible change when heated.

Irreversible: _____

Reversible: _____

**12** Is it safe to look directly at the Sun if you are wearing sunglasses? Why?

_____

_____

**13** Name a material that is a good thermal insulator, and a material that is a thermal conductor.

Thermal insulator: _____

Thermal conductor: _____

1 mark

1 mark

**14** Explain what happens if bicarbonate of soda and vinegar are mixed together.

_____

_____

2 marks

**15** Why is it always a good idea to repeat a scientific enquiry?

_____

1 mark

**16** The amount of water in clouds becomes so great that it falls to the ground as rain, snow or hail.

What is the name of the process described by the sentence above?

_____

1 mark

**17** Young children often believe that the Sun is moving across the sky during the day and that it goes down at night. Explain why the Sun appears to move and what happens to it at night time.

_____

_____

_____

2 marks

**18** Describe how a shadow is formed.

_____

_____

2 marks

# Contact Forces

## Challenge 1

1   Circle the underlined correct words to complete the sentences.

Forces are pushes and pulls, which are measured in <u>Newtons/ centimetres</u>. When forces are <u>balanced/unbalanced</u>, they can make objects move.

2 marks

2   What is the force that acts against the movement of an object travelling through water? Circle **one**.

Magnetism          Friction          Water resistance

1 mark

3   **True** or **false**? Air resistance can be reduced by changing the shape of the object travelling through the air. _____

1 mark

Marks.......... /4

## Challenge 2

1   A car's tyres are specially designed to 'grip' the road so that the wheels don't slide. What force is acting when the tyres are gripping the road?

_____

1 mark

2   On icy days, special trucks apply grit (rock salt) to the roads and pavements. Why might it be necessary to do this?

_____

_____

2 marks

3   The shape of a race car means that it can move quickly through the air. What is the name given to objects that are shaped in this way?

_____

1 marks

Marks.......... /4

# Contact Forces

**Challenge 3**

1 A man is riding his bike along a flat road.

a) What force is keeping the bike moving? Where does the force come from?

_____

_____

2 marks

b) Other than gravity, what forces act against the bike's movement? Explain the effect of these forces.

_____

_____

_____

3 marks

c) Why can the bike continue to move, even with these forces acting against it?

_____

_____

2 marks

d) The man stops pedalling and comes to a stop at the end of the road. What has happened to the forces acting on the bike to make it stop?

_____

_____

1 mark

e) The bike referred to above is a racing bike, which has smooth, thin tyres. The man also has a mountain bike, with wide, rough tyres. Why might the bikes need different types of tyres?

_____

_____

3 marks

f) In what other way might a racing bike be different from a mountain bike?

_____

_____

1 mark

Marks.........../12

Total marks ............ /20

How am I doing?

67

# Magnets and Gravity

## Challenge 1

1   How do gravity and the force from magnets differ from most other forces? Tick **one**.

They don't push or pull ☐   They don't affect objects at all ☐

They can act from a distance ☐   They need contact ☐

1 mark

2   **True** or **false**? Magnetic force is strongest at the ends of the magnet. _____

1 mark

3   Which of these objects would a magnet most likely attract? Circle **two.**

2 marks

Marks.......... /4

## Challenge 2

1   What are the two ends of a magnet called?

_____   _____

2 marks

2   The magnets below are attracted to one another. Label the second magnet to show which way round the poles must be.

**N        S**        ___    ___

1 mark

3   When a ball is kicked into the air, the force from the kick sends it upwards but then the ball falls back down. Why does the ball return to the ground?

_____

_____

2 marks

Marks.......... /5

# Magnets and Gravity

**Challenge 3**

1   The Earth's North and South Poles are magnetic, just like a bar magnet you can hold in your hand.

   **a)**  Name a device which uses the Earth's magnetic poles to help people to navigate.

   _____

   _1 mark_

   **b)**  The pointer in the device mentioned above is a magnet and one end of it always points North because it is attracted to the Earth's magnetic North Pole. On the diagram, label the north and south poles of the magnet in the device to show which way round they must be.

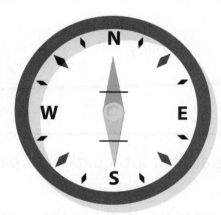

   _2 marks_

2   The Earth is a spherical (ball) shape. Explain why the people living on the Earth don't fall off.

   _____

   _____

   _2 marks_

3   Gravity is a powerful force. Give **one** example of how gravity affects things on Earth and another of how it affects things in the solar system.

   _____

   _____

   _2 marks_

Marks.......... /7

Total marks ............. /16          How am I doing?

# Levers, Pulleys and Gears

## Challenge 1

**1** Match the mechanism to what it uses.

| Lever | | Wheels with teeth around the edge |
| Gear | | A rope running over a wheel |
| Pulley | | A pivot and a long beam |

*3 marks*

**2** Which mechanism is used to collect water from a well? Circle the correct answer.

Lever          Pulley          Gear

*1 mark*

Marks........../4

## Challenge 2

**1** Mandy and Leo are playing at their local park. The park has a sand and water play area.

**a)** They are using buckets attached to ropes that run over a wheel to move the sand from the ground up on to a platform. What mechanism are they using?

_____

*1 mark*

**b)** Why does this mechanism make moving the sand easier?

_____

_____

*2 marks*

**c)** Mandy finds a large rock in the sand and wants to move it, but it is too heavy to lift. She pushes her spade under the rock and pushes down on the handle and can move the rock. What type of mechanism has she made? Why was she able to move the rock?

_____

_____

_____

*3 mark*

Marks........../6

# Levers, Pulleys and Gears

## Challenge 3

**1** Look at the image of the mechanism below.

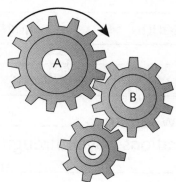

a) The gear labelled A is turning clockwise. Draw arrows to show the direction the other gears will turn.

b) Which gear will be turning the fastest?

_____

c) Which gear would need the most force to make a full turn?

_____

d) Give **two** examples of how gears can be used in everyday life.

_____

_____

2 marks

1 mark

1 mark

2 marks

Marks.......... /6

Total marks ............ /16          How am I doing?

# Making Sounds

## Challenge 1

**1** Use the words provided to complete these sentences.

| vibrates | sound | object or material |
|---|---|---|

| eardrum | medium |
|---|---|

_____ is made when an _____
_____. The vibrations travel through a
_____ to the _____ and sound is heard.

5 marks

**2** Tick **three** correct answers.

Sound can travel through:

the air ☐     water ☐     a vacuum ☐     a window ☐

3 marks

**3** **True** or **false**? The closer you are to the source of the sound, the louder it will be. _____

1 mark

Marks.......... /9

## Challenge 2

At the end of lunch at school, a teacher shakes and rings the bell to let the children know that play time is over.

Bell →

**1** How is the bell making a sound? Use the diagram of the bell to help you answer the question.

← Clapper

_____

_____

2 marks

**2** What medium did the sound travel through to get to the children's ears?

_____

1 mark

**3** Some children at the far side of the playground continue to play after the bell has rung. Why might they not have heard the bell?

_____

_____

2 marks

Marks.......... /5

# Making Sounds

## Challenge 3

**1** Luiz and Katie are at opposite ends of the playground railings. Katie taps on the railings and Luiz hears the sound. How is the sound made and why can Luiz hear it?

_____

_____

_____

**3 marks**

**2** Which two media would the sound be travelling through when Katie taps the railings?

_____

**2 marks**

**3** Katie taps the railings again, and Luiz notices that he hears the sound twice. Why might Luiz have heard the sound twice?

_____

_____

_____

**2 marks**

**4** Luiz believes that he would be able to hear the sound no matter how far he was from Katie. Katie thinks that the sound would eventually get too quiet to hear. Who is correct? Explain your answer.

_____

_____

_____

**2 marks**

Marks.......... /9

Total marks ............. /23          How am I doing?

73

# Pitch and Volume

## Challenge 1

**1** What is meant by the term volume when talking about sound?

_____

*1 mark*

**2** Circle the correct underlined words to complete the sentences.

**a)** Tapping gently on a triangle will make a <u>louder/fainter</u> sound.

**b)** Bigger vibrations have <u>more/less</u> energy and make a <u>louder/fainter</u> sound.

**c)** The <u>pitch/volume</u> of a sound describes how high or low the sound is.

*3 marks*

**3** Circle the objects below that are likely to make a high-pitched sound.

*3 marks*

Marks..........  /7

## Challenge 2

**1** Billy and Toby are both playing the xylophone. Billy taps the bars gently and Toby hits the bars harder. Whose xylophone will be making the louder sound? Why?

_____

_____

*2 marks*

**2** Billy prefers the sound that the shorter bars of the xylophone are making. Does Billy prefer high- or low-pitched sounds? How do you know?

_____

_____

*2 marks*

**3** Toby taps each bar on his xylophone, starting with the smallest and finishing with the largest. Describe what happens to the pitch of the sounds as he moves from the smallest to the largest bar. Explain your answer.

_____

_____

_____

*3 marks*

Marks.......... /7

# Pitch and Volume

## Challenge 3

Sarah has made a musical instrument out of an ice-cream tub and some elastic bands. All the bands are the same length but have different thicknesses. She places the bands around the container and plucks at them to make the sounds.

**1** Sarah predicts that the thicker bands will make a higher-pitched sound. Is her prediction likely to be correct? Explain your answer.

_____

_____

3 marks

**2** What has Sarah done that helps to make this a fair test?

_____

1 mark

**3** Sarah knows that higher-pitched sounds have a higher frequency. She tests the frequency of two different bands – the thickest and the thinnest. The sound waves are shown to the right.

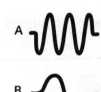

**a)** Which sound wave belongs to the thinner band?

_____

1 mark

**b)** Sarah tests a third band of medium thickness. Draw what you predict the sound wave will look like in the space below.

1 mark

Marks.......... /6

Total marks ............ /20

How am I doing?

# Making Circuits

**1** Draw a line from each device and appliance to show whether it runs on mains electricity or a battery.

| Mains electricity | | | Battery |
|---|---|---|---|

| torch | washing machine | mobile phone | television | freezer |
|---|---|---|---|---|

*5 marks*

**2** **True** or **false**? A circuit must be complete for it to work.

_____

*1 mark*

**3** Complete the sentence:

| component | energy | switch | light |
|---|---|---|---|

A battery provides the _____ for a circuit.

*1 mark*

Marks.......... /7

**1** Look at the circuit diagram below. Label the battery, a wire and the bulb.

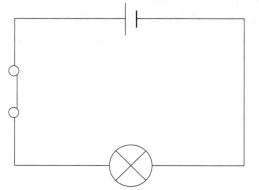

*3 marks*

**2** Draw the symbol for a motor.

*1 mark*

Marks.......... /4

# Making Circuits

**1**   Look at the picture of an electrical circuit.

**a)**   Draw a circuit diagram to represent the picture in the space above.

1 mark

**b)**   Explain why the buzzer in this circuit will work.

_____

1 mark

**2**   Look at the pictures below.

**A**    **B**    **C**

**a)**   Place a tick next to the picture in which the bulb will light.

1 mark

**b)**   Explain why the bulb will not light in each of the other two pictures.

_____

_____

1 mark

Marks......... /4

**Total marks** ............. /15                How am I doing?

# Breaking Circuits

## Challenge 1

1   Which component is often added to a circuit to stop and start the flow of electricity?

a buzzer ☐                 a bulb ☐

a switch ☐                 a motor ☐

1 mark

2   Place a tick by each of the objects below which are conductors of electricity.

2 marks

3   What is the opposite of a conductor of electricity?

_____

1 mark

Marks.......... /4

## Challenge 2

1   Look at the image of an electrical plug. Explain why part of it is metal and part plastic.

_____

_____

_____

_____

2 marks

2   a)  Draw the symbol for a switch that is 'off'.

b)  Draw the symbol for a switch that is 'on'.

| off | on |
|-----|-----|
|     |     |

2 marks

Marks.......... /4

# Breaking Circuits

## Challenge 3

**1** Look at the circuit diagrams below.

Say whether the buzzer will sound or not sound in each circuit.

**a)**

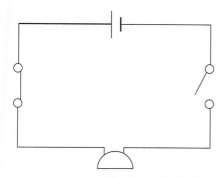

_____

1 mark

**b)**

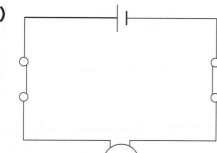

_____

1 mark

**c)**

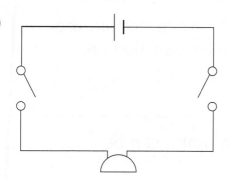

_____

1 mark

**2** Give a brief explanation of how a switch can make or break a circuit.

_____

_____

2 marks

Marks.........../5

**Total marks** ............. /13

How am I doing?

# Cells in Circuits

## Challenge 1

**1** What does a cell (battery) do in a circuit?

_____

1 mark

**2** Draw the symbol for a battery in a circuit.

1 mark

**3** Give **two** ways in which batteries could make the same bulb in a circuit brighter.

_____

_____

2 marks

Marks.......... /4

## Challenge 2

**1** The pupils are making model cars. They want a motor to turn the wheels and a buzzer to sound when the model is switched on.

What components do they need?

_____

4 marks

**2** Draw a circuit diagram for a circuit in which a motor can be switched on and off.

2 marks

Marks.......... /6

# Cells in Circuits

**Challenge 3**

**1** **a)** Draw a circuit in which there is a battery, a bulb and a motor. A switch is also needed which will make the motor turn and the bulb light up when the switch is on.

2 marks

**b)** Draw the circuit again, this time adding something which will make the bulb brighter when the switch is on.

1 mark

**2** What is the danger of adding more batteries to a circuit?

_____

_____

1 mark

Marks.........../4

Total marks ............./14

How am I doing?

81

1 Describe the difference between the way igneous and metamorphic rock is formed.

_____

_____

2 marks

2 A black and white cat has a litter of six kittens. Some of them are black and white and look like mum, but others are ginger or have ginger spots and white patches.

a) Why don't all the kittens look like their mum? What is it called when animals have differences like this?

_____

_____

2 marks

b) From the description of the kittens, predict what the dad cat might have looked like. Explain why you have made this prediction.

_____

_____

1 mark

3 For her science project, Jessica has designed and made a rocket and a rocket launcher. She places the rocket onto the launcher and pushes down on a plunger, which pumps air into the rocket. The rocket shoots into the air and then falls back to the ground.

a) What kind of force makes the rocket shoot up into the air and where does it come from?

_____

_____

2 marks

b) Why does the rocket fall back to the ground?

_____

_____

2 marks

**4** Ava and Samira are at the cinema to watch a new film.

**a)** Describe how they see the film.

_____

_____ 2 marks

**b)** Explain how the sound travels from the speakers to their ears.

_____

_____

_____ 2 marks

**5** Alfie loves playing his guitar, and practises every day after school. Before he starts playing, he checks the strings and sometimes has to tighten or loosen them.

What would tightening the guitar strings do to the sound the strings make?

_____ 1 mark

**6 a)** Explain the difference between a conductor and an insulator of electricity.

_____

_____ 2 marks

**b)** Give an example of an object which is used to conduct electricity.

_____ 1 mark

**c)** Give an example of an everyday object used to insulate electricity.

_____ 1 mark

**7** What type of mechanism does a watch use to make the hands move at different speeds? How do they work?

_____

_____ 2 marks

8    Look at the circuit diagram below.

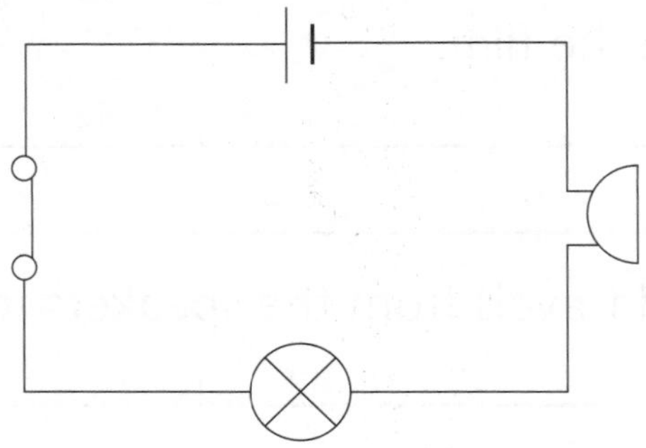

   a)   Name the other **two** components in the diagram:

        battery     switch     _____     _____

        *2 marks*

   b)   Explain the role of the switch in the circuit, and how it controls
        the other components.

        _____

        _____

        *2 marks*

9    What is the difference between an invertebrate and a vertebrate?

     _____

     *1 mark*

10   Explain what happens during the process of condensation in the
     water cycle.

     _____

     _____

     *2 marks*

11   Explain the difference between soluble and insoluble materials.

     _____

     _____

     *2 marks*

12   Inside a volcano, rocks and minerals get so hot that they melt and
     form magma. When this magma cools, it forms a type of rock.
     Which type of rock is formed when magma cools?

     _____

     *1 mark*

Marks........ /30

84